Oxford International Resources

7

Science

Workbook

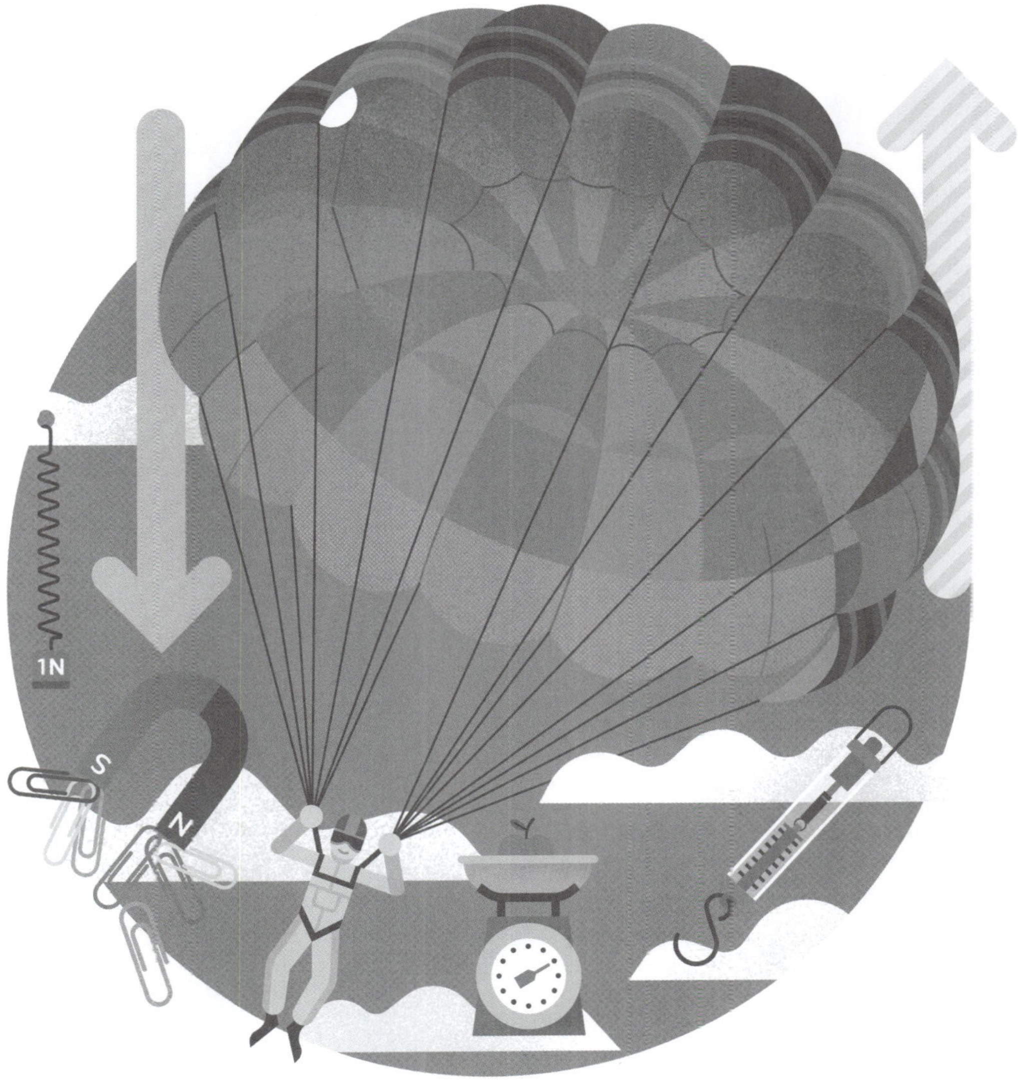

Jo Locke
Anna Harris
Alyssa Fox-Charles

OXFORD
UNIVERSITY PRESS

OXFORD
UNIVERSITY PRESS

Great Clarendon Street, Oxford, OX2 6DP, United Kingdom

Oxford University Press is a department of the University of Oxford. It furthers the University's objective of excellence in research, scholarship, and education by publishing worldwide. Oxford is a registered trade mark of Oxford University Press in the UK and in certain other countries.

First published in 2026

British Library Cataloguing in Publication Data

Data available

ISBN 978-1-382-07219-9

10 9 8 7 6 5 4 3 2 1

The manufacturing process conforms to the environmental regulations of the country of origin.

Printed in India by Multivista Global Pvt. Ltd

The manufacturer's authorised representative in the EU for product safety is Oxford University Press España S.A. of El Parque Empresarial San Fernando de Henares, Avenida de Castilla, 2 – 28830 Madrid (www.oup.es/en or product.safety@oup.com). OUP España S.A. also acts as importer into Spain of products made by the manufacturer.

Acknowledgements
Written by Jo Locke, Anna Harris, Alyssa Fox-Charles

The publisher and authors would like to thank the following for permission to use photographs and other copyright material:

Cover: Angel Svoboda

Artist: QBS Learning, Aptara Inc., Six Red Marbles, Kamae Design, IFA Design, GreenGate Publishing, Phoenix Photosetting, Wearset Ltd, Barking Dog Art, Tech Set Ltd, HL Studios, Integra Software Services, Hardlines, Tech Graphics, Pantek Arts Ltd, Nelson Thornes Ltd, David Russell Illustration, Peter Bull Art Studio, Mark Walker, Erwin Haya, Matt Ward, Martina Farrow, James Stayte, Trystan Mitchell, Edward Fullick, Matthew Bass, Stewart Miller, Michal Bednarski, Jeffrey Bowles, Roger Courthold, Mike Ogden, Jeff Edwards, Russell Walker, Clive Goodyer, Jamie Sneddon, Kathy Baxendale, Anthony Rule, Stéphan Theron, Robin Edmonds, John Hallett, Lisa Hunt, Caron Painter, Claire Rollet, Martin Sanders, Rory Walker and Oxford University Press.

Photos: p53: CNRI / SCIENCE PHOTO LIBRARY.

Every effort has been made to contact copyright holders of material reproduced in this book. Any omissions will be rectified in subsequent printings if notice is given to the publisher.

FSC www.fsc.org MIX Paper | Supporting responsible forestry FSC® C199630

Contents

1.1 Asking scientific questions

Gathering ideas

Learning objectives

- Develop an idea into a question that can be investigated
- Identify independent, dependent, and control variables
- Make a scientific prediction

Task

At each station in the classroom, you will find an object or objects.

For each station, answer Questions 1–3 and use your answers to complete the table on the next page.

1 Think of **three** questions you might like to find out.

2 Develop **one** of these ideas into a scientific question that can be investigated.

3 Identify the independent, dependent, and control variable(s) for this investigation.

Then choose **one** of your scientific questions and answer Question 4.

4 Write a prediction for what you think would happen if you carried out an investigation to answer this question.

Scientific question

____

Prediction

____

____

Station	**Ideas** (Think of three questions)	**Scientific questions** (Choose one that can be investigated)	Variables
A	**1** **2** **3**		Independent (**what you change**): Dependent (**what you measure**): Control (**what you keep the same**):
B	**1** **2** **3**		Independent: Dependent: Control:
C	**1** **2** **3**		Independent: Dependent: Control:

Support

Station	**Ideas** (Think of three questions)	**Scientific questions** (Choose one that can be investigated)	**Variables**
Example: a rubber band	**1** How far does the rubber band stretch? **2** Does the rubber band make a noise if I pluck it? **3** Can I use the rubber band to make a car move?	How far does the rubber band stretch when I apply a force?	Independent (**what you change**): force used Dependent (**what you measure**): distance rubber band stretches from starting position Control (**what you keep the same**): width of rubber band, type of rubber
A	**1** **2** **3**		Independent: Dependent: Control:
B	**1** **2** **3**		Independent: Dependent: Control:

1.2 Working safely

Bunsen burners

Learning objectives

- Recognize commonly used hazard symbols and their meanings
- Identify possible hazards in practical work
- Understand the purpose of a risk assessment

Questions

1 The Bunsen burner was named after Robert Bunsen.

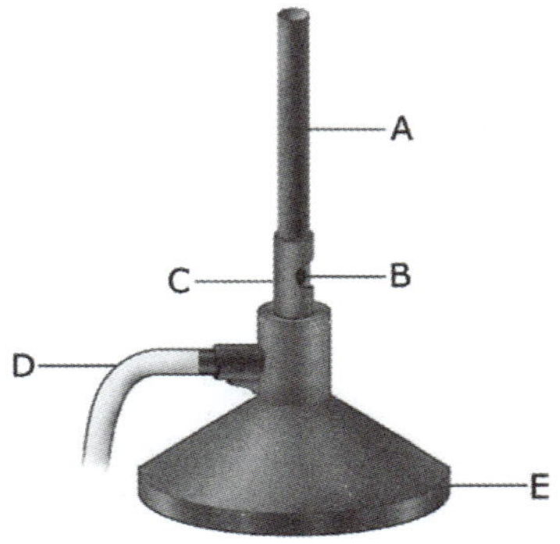

Using the diagram match the parts of the Bunsen burner with the letter.

Part		Label
1	barrel (tube)	C
2	air hole	D
3	base	E
4	collar (band)	A
5	gas hose	B

2 Which part of the Bunsen burner remains cool? ______________________________

3 The collar (band) can be moved to change how much air can mix with the gas. The position of the collar can produce three different flames.

a The Bunsen burner is burning with a yellow flame.

Is the air hole completely open, open in part, or closed? ______________________________

When would you use this type of flame? ______________________________

b The Bunsen Burner is burning with a pale blue flame.

Is the air hole completely open, open in part, or closed? ______________________________

When would you use this type of flame? ______________________________

c The Bunsen Burner is burning with a blue, roaring (strong) flame.

Is the air hole completely open, open in part, or closed? ______________________________

When would you use this type of flame? ______________________________

1.3 Planning investigations

What do you need?

Learning objectives

- Write a plan for a scientific investigation
- Identify the scientific equipment used to measure different quantities
- Take accurate measurements

Task

At each station:

1. Choose the most suitable equipment to make the measurement described.
2. Identify the units of measurement and add these to the table.
3. Think about any safety precautions you need. Write these down in your results table (there may not be any).
4. Take a reading.
5. To check your results, repeat the reading two more times.

Station	Equipment used	Reading 1	Reading 2	Reading 3	Any safety precautions?
A Volume of liquid in the beaker					
B Thickness of a pile of paper					
C Mass of a piece of cloth					
D Time taken for paper ball to fall 1 m					

Questions

1 **Station A:** Draw a 2D image of the measuring equipment.

2 **Station A:** Describe how you used the equipment to measure the volume of liquid. (Key words: *meniscus*, *parallax error*)

3 **Station B:** Describe how you used the equipment to measure the thickness of a pile of paper.

4 **Station C:** State the name of the equipment you used to measure the mass of a piece of cloth. Give a reason why you would not use bathroom scales to take this measurement.

5 **Station D:** Your results are probably different from those of other students in your class. Why do you think this might have happened?

Support

Station	Equipment used	Reading 1	Reading 2	Reading 3
A **Volume** of liquid in the beaker		cm^3	cm^3	cm^3
B **Thickness** of a pile of paper		mm	mm	mm
C **Mass** of a piece of cloth		g	g	g
D **Time** taken for crumpled paper to fall a vertical distance of 1 m		s	s	s

1.4 Recording data

Practical: Bouncing a ball

Learning objectives

- Design a results table
- Present data in a results table
- Calculate a mean from repeat measurements

Safety

- Try not to let balls roll on the floor.

Equipment and materials

- metre rule
- five different types of ball

Method

In this practical, you will investigate this question:
Does the type of ball affect how high it bounces when it is dropped 1 m from the ground?

1 Drop a ball from a height of 1 m, next to a metre ruler.

2 Measure the height the ball bounces (on its first bounce).

3 Repeat the measurement two more times.

4 Repeat steps **1–3** for a different type of ball.

Questions

1 Identify the **independent** variable.

___

2 Identify the **dependent** variable.

___

3 Name **two** variables you will **control**.

___

4 Design a results table to record your results (see the next page), before starting your practical.

Results

- Include a column for the **independent** variable.
- Include three columns for the **dependent** variable – you will repeat readings.
- Include a column for the **mean** of the readings.
- Each column heading includes the name of the variable and its unit.
- You need one row for each value of the independent variable.

5 Calculate the means for your results. Add these mean values to your results table.

6 State which type of ball bounced the highest.

____

Support

Questions

Does the type of ball affect how high it bounces when it is dropped 1 m from the ground?

1 Choose the **independent** variable: type of ball / height of bounce / height it falls.

2 Choose the **dependent** variable: type of ball / height of bounce / height it falls.

3 Choose a variable you will **control**: type of ball / height of bounce / height it falls.

4 Complete the headers in the results table below.

				Mean bounce height in cm
	First reading	Second reading	Third reading	

5 Carry out the experiment and record your readings in your table. Work out the **mean** of your results by:

- adding together the three readings for each type of ball
- dividing your answer by three (as there are three measurements).

1.5 Presenting data

How many wild birds?

Learning objectives

- Classify data as continuous, discrete, or categorical
- Present data in a chart or graph

Task 1

A birdwatcher kept a record of the number of wild birds that visited their garden during a three-hour period. Their results are shown below.

Bird species	Number of birds seen
robin	5
blue tit	2
pigeon	1
sparrow	3
thrush	1

Use the graph paper to plot the data as a bar chart.

Task 2

A gardener investigated how fertilizer affects how quickly tomato plants grow. Their results are shown below.

Mass of fertilizer in g	Increase in plant height after 10 days in mm
0	6
2	12
4	16
6	15
8	8

Use the graph below to plot the data as a line graph.

Task 3

The local council wanted to work out how much of the recycling they collected was made of various materials. The data they collected is summarized in the table below.

Type of recycling	Percentage of recycling	Pie chart segment angle in °
cardboard	50	180
glass	25	90
metal	8	30
plastic	17	60

They want to show their data as a pie chart to place on a recycling poster.

Use the segment angles from the table to plot your pie chart in the space below.

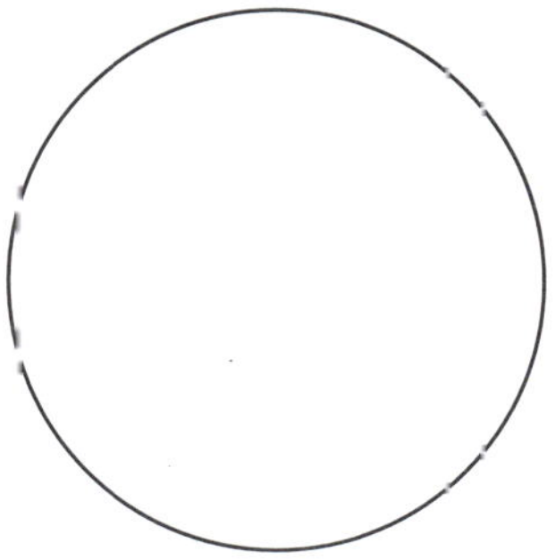

Support

Task 1

Record the results in the bar chart below.

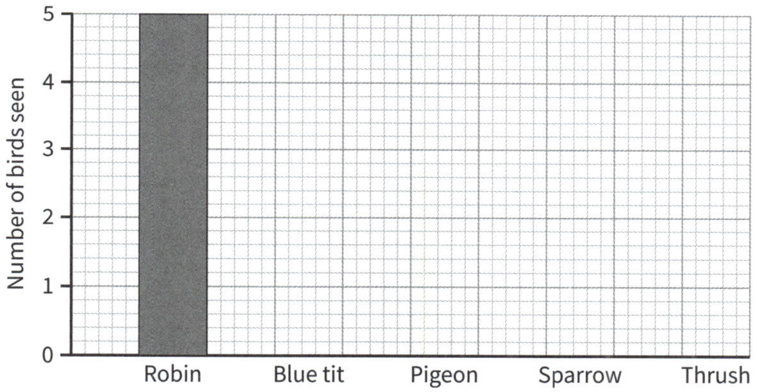

Task 2

Use the axes below to plot the data as a line graph.

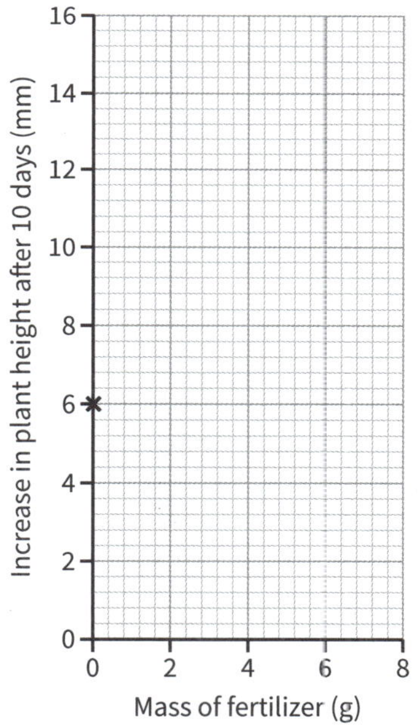

Task 3

Use the segment angles to plot your pie chart. The result for glass has been done for you.

Tip: Turn the page to draw the next segment so the line you are measuring from points towards 0 on your protractor.

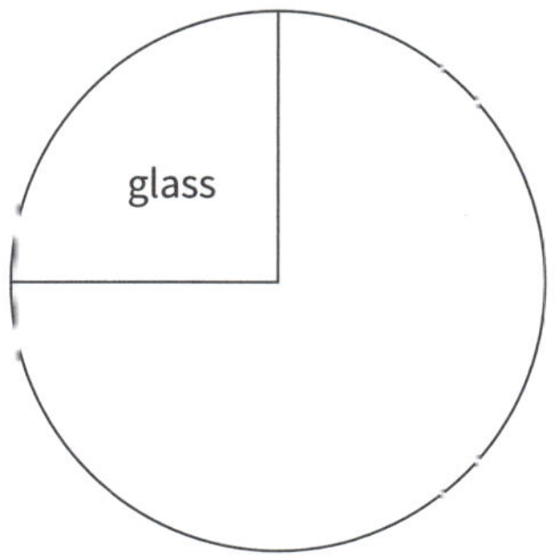

1.6 Analysing data

Identifying patterns

Learning objectives

- Identify patterns or trends in data using a graph or chart
- Interpret data to draw conclusions

Task

You have been provided with two sets of data. Plot a line graph for the data using the grids. Remember:

- The independent variable goes on the *x*-axis and the dependent variable on the *y*-axis.
- Choose the scale so the numbers go up in equal steps.
- You do not always have to start the scale for the *y*-axis at zero.
- Label both axes, including units.

Add a line of best fit:

- Your line should be straight, or a smooth curve.
- It should pass through, or very close to, as many points as possible.

Write a conclusion. Describe the pattern shown in the data.

Table 1

Volume of water in cm^3	Height of water in measuring cylinder in cm
20	2
40	4
60	6
80	8
100	10

Graph 1

Conclusion 1

Table 2

Angle of incident light ray in °	Angle of reflected light ray in °
10	12
20	20
30	28
40	42
50	50

Graph 2

Conclusion 2

1.7 Evaluating data

WORKING SCIENTIFICALLY

Choosing the best method

Learning objectives

- Describe the stages in evaluating data
- Suggest ways to improve a practical investigation

Task 1

Here are two accounts written by students who wanted to know how far different balls travelled when hit with a tennis racket.

Experiment 1

I bounced the table tennis ball, the squash ball, and the tennis ball, then hit them. I threw the golf ball and the snooker ball in the air, then hit them.

I stood in different places after the snooker ball broke a window. I tested the tennis ball three times and the other balls once.

The tennis ball went furthest. I decided this by looking. I think my test went well.

Experiment 2

I tried bouncing the balls but it didn't work for all of the balls. So I threw each ball in the air and hit it medium-hard. I practised a few times. Then I took a set of results, and took measurements for each ball three times.

I stood in the same place each time and measured the distances with a tape measure. I calculated the mean of the results.

The tennis ball went furthest. I think my test went well.

Summarize the key differences between the experiments in the table below.

Experiment 1	Experiment 2

Questions

1 State which experiment would give better results. Explain your answer.

---

2 Suggest **three** ways to improve the other experiment.

Task 2

Force used in N	Length of rubber band in cm	
	Measurement 1	Measurement 2
1	10.0	10.2
2	11.1	11.0
3	12.0	12.2
4	18.8	13.5
5	14.2	14.1

Questions

1 Circle any anomalies.

2 Describe the spread of the data.

---

3 Comment on the repeatability of the data.

---

4 Suggest **two** ways the quality of the data could be improved.

Support

Two students carried out an experiment into which type of ball travels furthest when hit with a tennis racket. They tested a tennis ball, a snooker ball, a golf ball, a small football, and a table tennis ball. Each student used a different method.

Method: Student 1

- I bounced three of the balls, and then hit them with the tennis racket.
- Two balls didn't bounce, so I threw them into the air and then hit them.
- I stood in different places each time so I didn't annoy anyone else.
- I tested the tennis ball three times, but only had time to test the other balls once.
- I looked to see which ball went furthest.

Method: Student 2

- I threw each ball into the air, and then hit it medium-hard each time.
- I stood in the same place each time before hitting the balls.
- I measured the distances travelled with a tape measure.
- I tested each ball three times, then worked out an average distance travelled.

1 Write the differences between the experiments in the table below.

Experiment 1	Experiment 2

2 Give **two** improvements for **Student 1**'s experiment that would give better quality results.

1.1 Observing cells

Practical: Discovering the microscope

Learning objectives

- Describe how to use a microscope to look at very small objects
- Calculate the total magnification used to look at an object

Safety

- Take care when lifting microscopes and when using glass items.
- Ask a responsible adult to brush up broken glass immediately.

Equipment and materials

- microscope
- glass slides prepared with samples
- objects to look at under a microscope, such as insect wings or petals

Task

1 Label the microscope. Add a sentence describing what each part does.

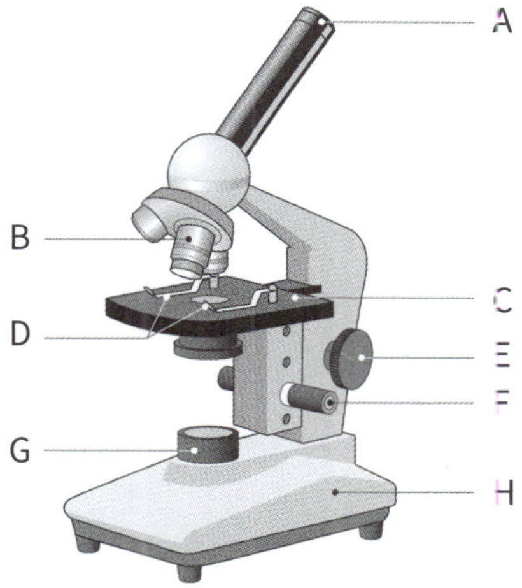

A ______________________________

____

B ______________________________

____

C ______________________________

____

D ______________________________

____

E ______________________________

____

F ______________________________

____

G ______________________________

____

H ______________________________

____

2 Choose one of the objects you looked at under the microscope. Draw what you saw below.

3 Calculate the total magnification you used to look at this object.

total magnification = eyepiece lens magnification × objective lens magnification

total magnification = ____________ × ____________

total magnification = × ____________

Support

Use the names of the microscope parts below to label your diagram.

- eyepiece lens
- base
- stage
- light source
- fine focus
- coarse focus
- objective lens
- stage clips

Now choose what each part does.

- platform on which you place the object or slide being looked at
- stops the microscope from moving
- hold microscope slide in place
- provides light to see the image
- lens you look through; magnifies the image
- nearly focuses the image
- lens you choose to magnify the image
- focuses the object in sharp detail

1.2 Plant and animal cells

BIOLOGY

Practical: Observing plant and animal cells

Learning objectives

- Describe what each part of a cell does
- Compare the parts of plant and animal cells
- Use a microscope to look at plant and animal cells

Onion cells

Safety

- Take care when lifting microscopes and when using glass items.
- Beware of broken glass. Ask a responsible adult to brush up broken glass immediately.
- Avoid getting iodine solution on your skin.
- Wear safety glasses.

Equipment and materials

- microscope
- glass slide and coverslip
- forceps
- iodine solution and pipette
- onion slice
- safety glasses

Method

1 Remove one of the onion layers.
2 Use forceps to carefully pull off the skin on the inside of the onion layer.

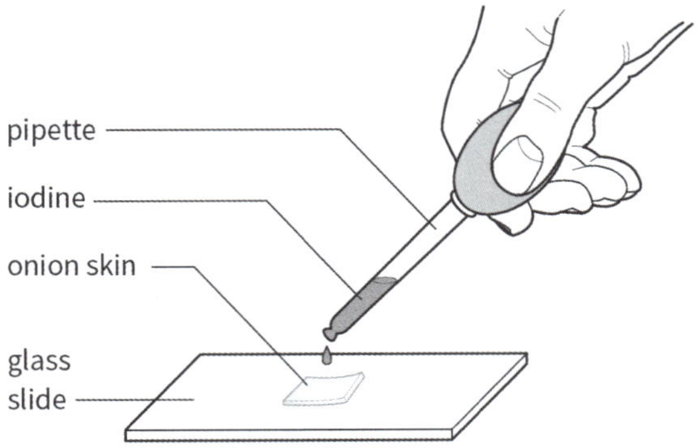

3 Place the onion skin onto a glass slide. Use the forceps to keep the onion skin flat on the glass slide.
4 Use a pipette to add one or two drops of dilute iodine solution on top of the onion skin.
5 Place a coverslip on top of the skin.
6 Look at your slide using a microscope.

Cheek cells

Safety

- Take care when lifting microscopes and when using glass items.
- Beware of broken glass. Ask a responsible adult to brush up broken glass immediately.
- Avoid getting methylene blue solution on your skin.
- Wear safety glasses.

Equipment and materials

- microscope
- glass slide and coverslip
- forceps
- methylene blue solution and pipette
- cotton swabs
- safety glasses
- safety gloves

Method

1. Gently brush the inside of your cheek with a clean cotton swab.
2. Roll the cotton swab across the centre of the microscope slide.
3. Wear gloves and use a pipette to add a drop of methylene blue solution onto the cheek cells.
4. Place a coverslip on top.
5. Look at your slide using a microscope.

Results

Draw a labelled diagram of an onion cell and a cheek cell in the space below.

Questions

1 Add a tick (✓) in the table to identify which parts you can see in each cell. You may not be able to see some parts under a microscope.

Part	Seen in onion cell	Seen in cheek cell	Function (job)
cell membrane			
cell wall			
nucleus			
cytoplasm			
mitochondria			
vacuole			
chloroplast			

2 Add a sentence to describe what each part does in the table.

3 Onion cells are plant cells, but they do not contain chloroplasts. Explain why.

____

____

Support

Tips

- Use a sharp pencil for your drawing.
- Use a ruler to add label lines pointing to the main parts in your diagram.
- Add the names of the cell parts to your diagram. You should be able to see the nucleus, cell membrane, and cytoplasm in both cells. You should also be able to see the cell wall in the onion cell.

Use the descriptions below to add what the cell parts do to your results table.

- where photosynthesis occurs
- makes the cell stronger and provides support
- controls what enters and leaves a cell
- contains cell sap and keeps the cell firm
- controls the cell and contains genetic material
- where respiration occurs
- 'jelly-like' substance where chemical reactions occur

1.3 Specialized cells

Model cells

Learning objectives

- Describe the function (job) of specialized cells
- Describe the features of specialized plant cells
- Describe the features of specialized animal cells

Task

1 Research the cell you have been given.
2 Gather any materials you require to make your model of the specialized cell. Remember to make it large enough to label all its key features, as well as the cell parts found in all cells.
3 Make your model of a specialized cell.
4 Add labels describing the cell's function (job) and adaptations.
5 Record information about your cell in the results table.
6 Visit other students' models of specialized cells, and add the information to your results table.

Results

Specialized cell	Plant or animal?	Function (job)	Diagram	Adaptations	Challenge: How do the adaptations allow it to perform its function?

Support

Below are the names, diagrams, and functions (jobs) of some specialized plant and animal cells. They are not in the correct order. Photocopy this page. Cut out the boxes, sort them, and stick them on to your table.

root hair cell		carry electrical impulses around the body	long and thin, connections at each end
skeletal muscle cell	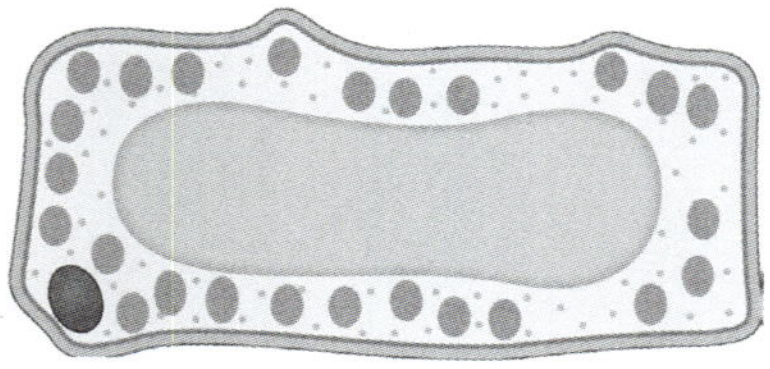	take in water and nutrients from soil	contains haemoglobin, no nucleus, curve in on both sides
leaf cell	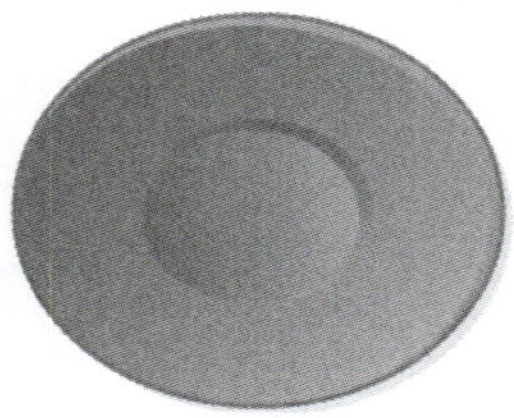	carry out photosynthesis	many mitochondria, long protein filaments
nerve cell	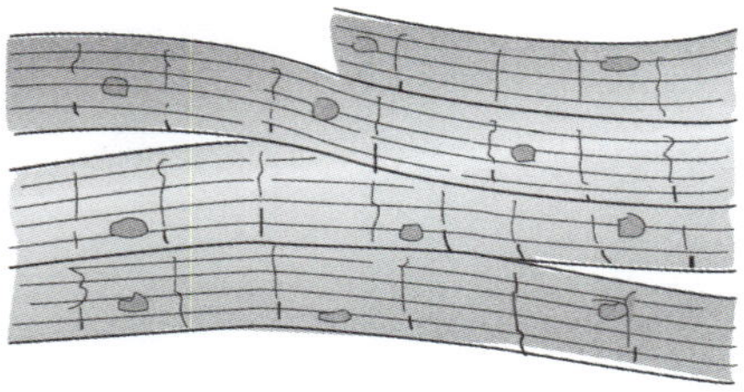	transport oxygen	large surface area, no chloroplasts
red blood cell	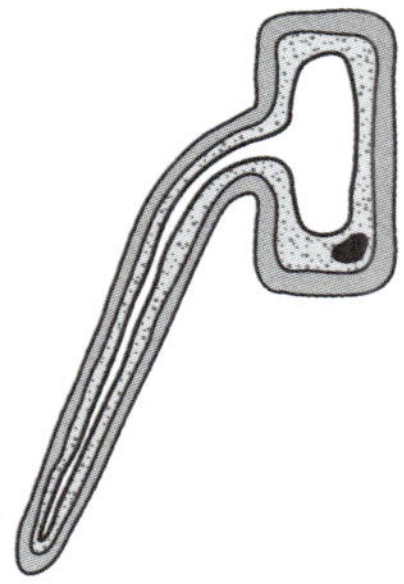	contracts to cause movement	long and thin, packed with chloroplasts

1.4 Diffusion in cells

BIOLOGY

Practical: Observing diffusion

Learning objectives

- Name some substances that move into cells and out of cells
- Describe the process of diffusion
- Describe examples of diffusion

Safety

- Take care when using glass items.
- Wash hands after lifting the coloured agar gel with the forceps.

Equipment and materials

- 250 cm^3 beaker (measuring cup)
- 100 cm^3 measuring cylinder
- water
- agar gel with coloured dye
- forceps
- stopwatch
- white sheet of paper

Method

1. Measure out 100 cm^3 of cold water using a measuring cylinder and pour it into the 250 cm^3 beaker.
2. Stand your beaker on a white sheet of paper.
3. Collect a cube (3D square) of coloured agar gel using forceps.
4. Place the coloured agar gel into the beaker of water.
5. Write down what you see happening in the beaker after 0, 5, 10, and 25 minutes in the results table.

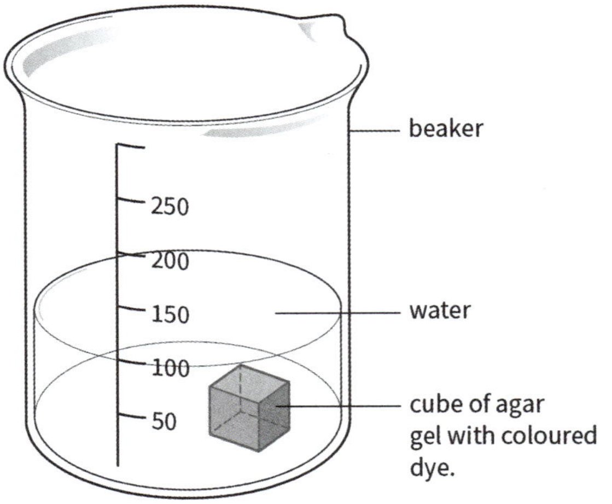

Questions

1 What did you observe (notice) about the colour of the water?

____

____

2 What did you observe about the gel? Does its shape or size change?

____

____

3 Name and describe the process you saw happening.

____

____

____

____

Support

When you are asked to make an *observation*, you are being asked to look carefully at what happens.

Think about:

- Does the gel change shape?
- Does the gel change size?
- Does anything happen to the colour of the water?

Use the sentences below to complete your conclusion.

Over time, dye comes out of the ____________

The colour goes into the ____________

The colour then ____________ out.

This process is called ____________

1.5 Unicellular organisms

Practical: Observing amoebas and euglenas

Learning objectives

- Describe a unicellular organism
- Describe the features of an amoeba
- Describe the features of a euglena

Safety

- Take care when lifting microscopes.
- Take care when using glass items.
- Avoid contact with living organisms.
- Wash your hands after preparing the slides.

Equipment and materials

- microscope
- cavity slide and coverslip
- pipettes
- suspensions of amoeba and euglena
- solution to slow cell movement

Method

1. Take a cavity slide and make sure the dip is on the upper surface.
2. Use a pipette to add one small drop of the amoeba suspension to the centre of the dip.
3. Use a clean pipette to add a small drop of the solution to the centre of the same dip and allow the two drops to mix naturally.
4. Place a coverslip over the dip of the slide.
5. Place the slide on the microscope and look for the amoeba.
6. Draw a diagram to show what you can see through the microscope.
7. Repeat the process using the euglena suspension.

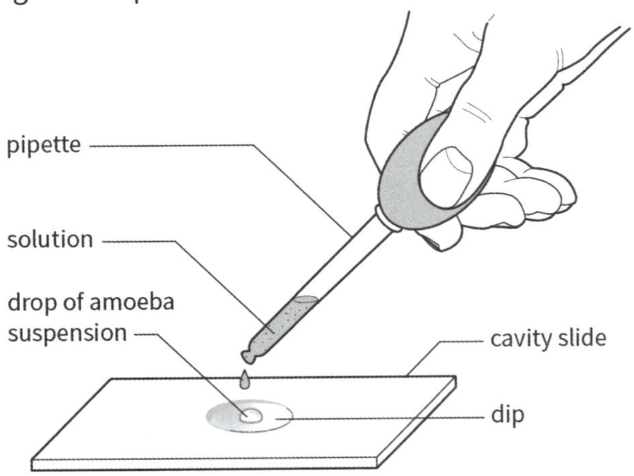

Results

For each slide, draw a large, labelled diagram of the cell you see down the microscope in the space below.

Questions

1 Complete the table. Identify the structures (listed below) that are in each type of cell.

nucleus   cytoplasm   cell membrane   chloroplasts   pseudopod
contractile vacuole   eye spot   flagellum   food vacuole

Found in amoeba	Found in euglena	Found in both

2 Apart from the structures, describe one other difference you observed between amoeba and euglena.

3 Which of the cells was easier to see? Suggest why.

4 Describe the process by which amoebas and euglenas reproduce.

Support

Amoebas

Tips for drawing an amoeba as seen through a microscope:

- Use as much of the space provided as possible.
- Use a sharp pencil.
- Draw with simple, clear lines (not sketchy lines).
- Use a ruler for label lines.

You should be able to label the: **cell membrane**, **cytoplasm**, **nucleus**.

Euglenas

This is a diagram of a euglena. Label as many parts of the cell as you can.

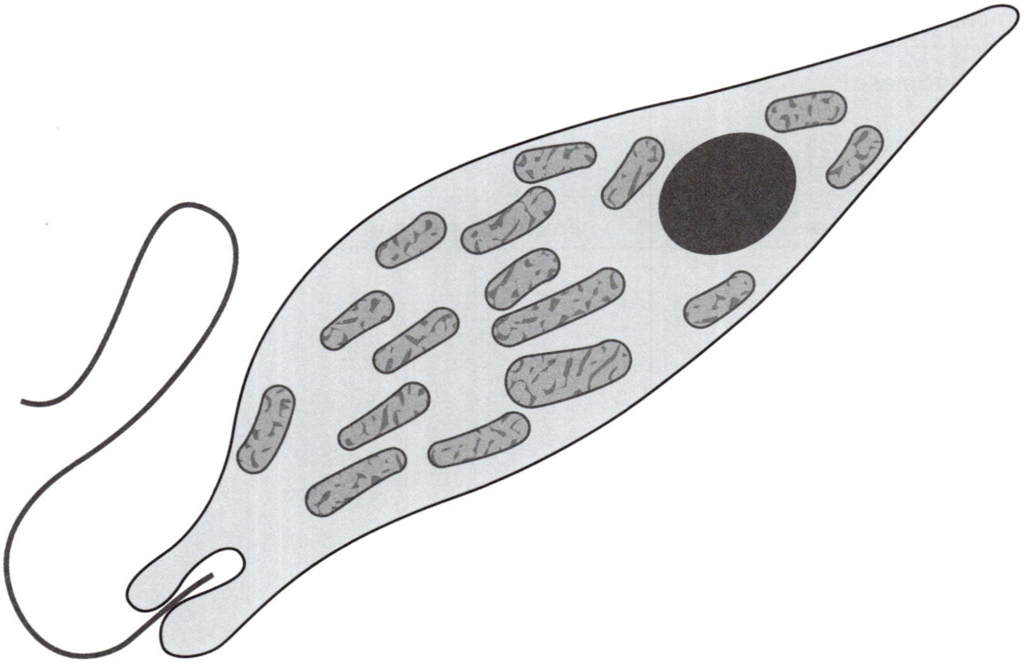

2.1 Levels of organization

Organizing a body

Learning objectives

- Define a tissue, an organ, and an organ system
- Describe the levels of organization in a multicellular organism

Task 1

1 State what all living things are made of.

____

2 Name **three** parts found in all cells.

____

3 Name **three** examples of specialized cells.

____

4 Define the word *tissue*.

____

5 State the name of a group of tissues working together.

____

6 Define the phrase *organ system*.

____

Task 2

Research an organ system. Find out its main functions (jobs) and examples of organs found in the system. Present your information to other pairs in the class.

Complete the table on the next page using your own research and from listening to other groups.

Organ system	Main functions (jobs)	Organs found in the system

Support

1 Match the levels of organization with their function.

tissue	group of tissues working together
organ system	group of cells working together
organ	group of organs working together

2 Write the correct name for each level of organization in this example. Choose from the words below.

cell	organ	organ system	tissue

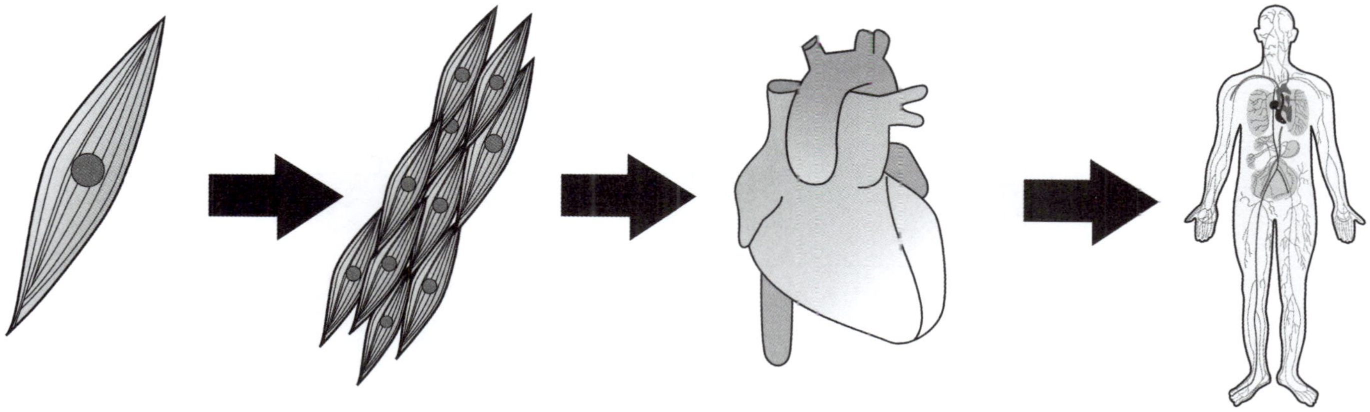

______ ______ ______ ______

3 Name **two** specialized cells.

______

4 Name these organ systems.

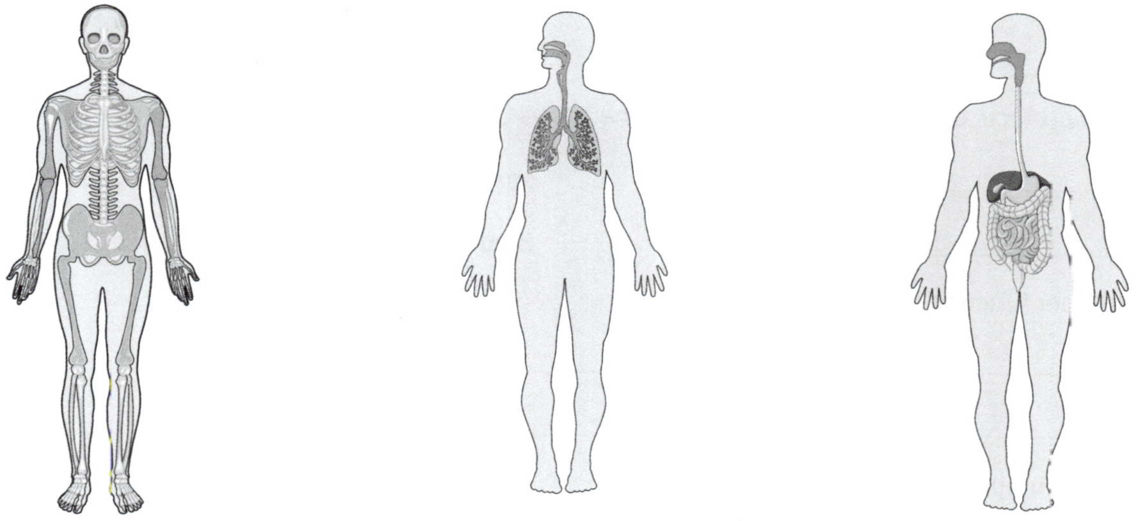

______ ______ ______

2.2 Skeleton

Build your own skeleton

Learning objectives

- Label the main bones in the human skeleton
- Describe the structure of a bone
- Describe the functions of the skeletal system

Task

Label the below diagram of the skeleton.

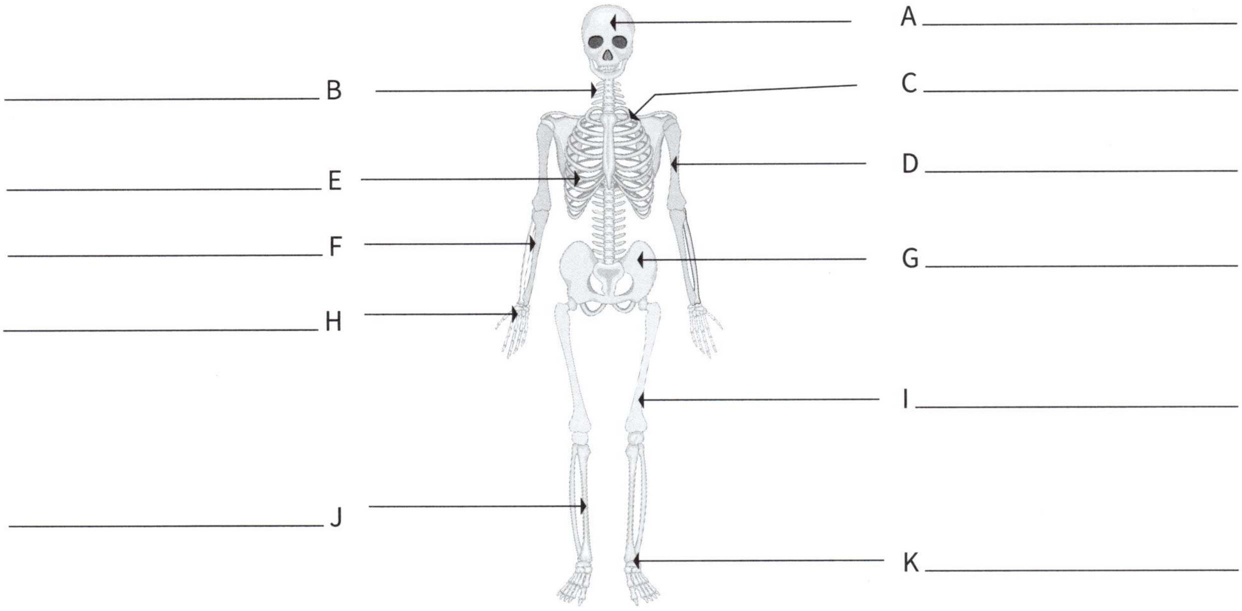

Questions

1 The skeleton protects organs. State the names of the bones that protect the following organs.

lungs: ______________________ **spinal cord:** ______________________

brain: ______________________ **heart:** ______________________

2 Name **two** other functions of the skeleton.

____

____

3 Describe the structure of bone.

____

____

Support

1 Below is a list of parts of a skeleton. Write these parts next to the correct label on the diagram of a skeleton.

tibia and fibula	pelvis	skull	ribs
femur	wrist bones	ankle bones	vertebrae
humerus	radius and ulna	clavicle	

2 Choose words from the list to complete the sentences about the functions (jobs) of the skeleton.

blood	move	protects	supports

The skeleton ______________________________ the body and holds your organs in place.

It ______________________________ important organs like the brain.

The skeleton helps the body to ______________________________.

Some bones also make ______________________________ cells.

2.3 Movement: joints

Practical: Measuring muscle strength

Learning objectives

- Describe the role of joints in movement
- Describe the structure of a joint
- Describe how to measure the force exerted (applied) by different muscles

Safety

- Ensure scales are positioned safely away from the edges of tables.

Equipment and materials

- newton scales

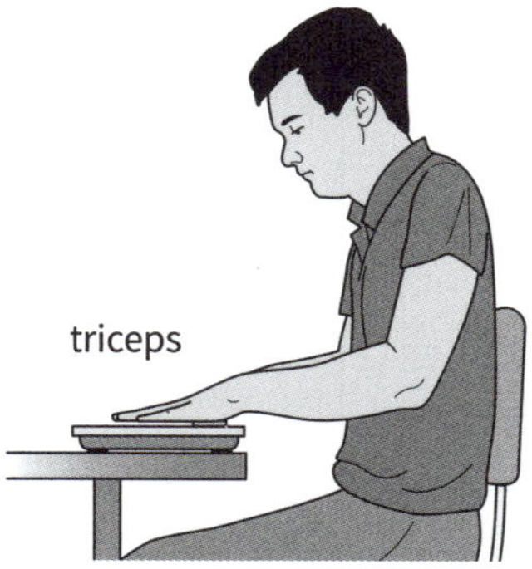

Method

To measure the strength of your triceps

1 Place the scales on top of the table.
2 Push down as hard as you can on the scales.
3 Record the force applied in newtons.

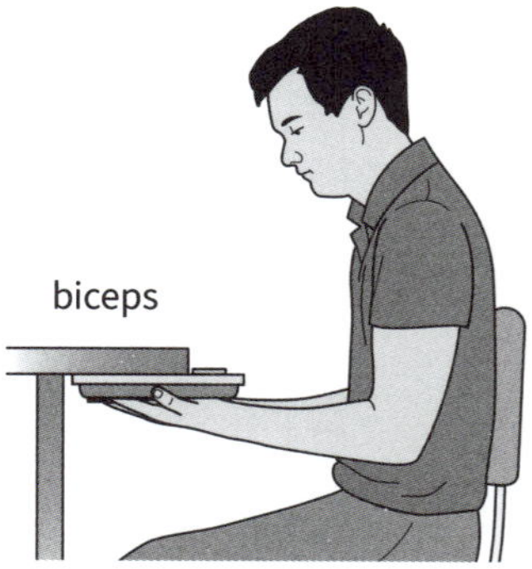

To measure the strength of your biceps

1 Hold the scales under the table.
Ask another student to sit on the table to make sure it does not move. Push up as hard as you can.
2 Record the force used in newtons.

Results

Design a results table in the space below to record your measurements.

Questions

1 Identify which of your muscles was the strongest.

____

2 Movement occurs in the skeleton at joints. Label the below diagram of the parts of the joint.

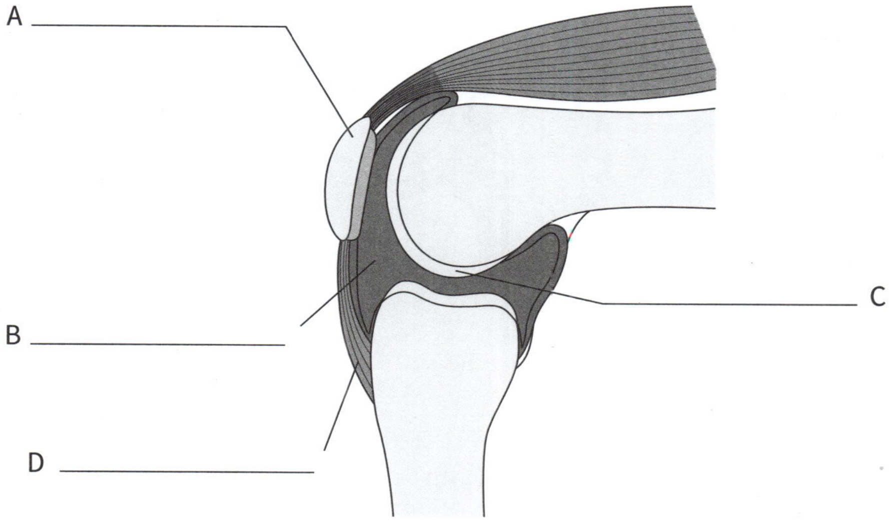

3 Complete the table to describe the function of the structures in a joint.

Structure	Function (job)
ligament	
cartilage	
fluid (liquid)	

Support

1 Use this table to record your muscle strength (force in newtons).

Muscle group	Force in N
triceps	
biceps	

2 Use the words below to label the structures in a joint.

bone	ligament	fluid (liquid)	cartilage

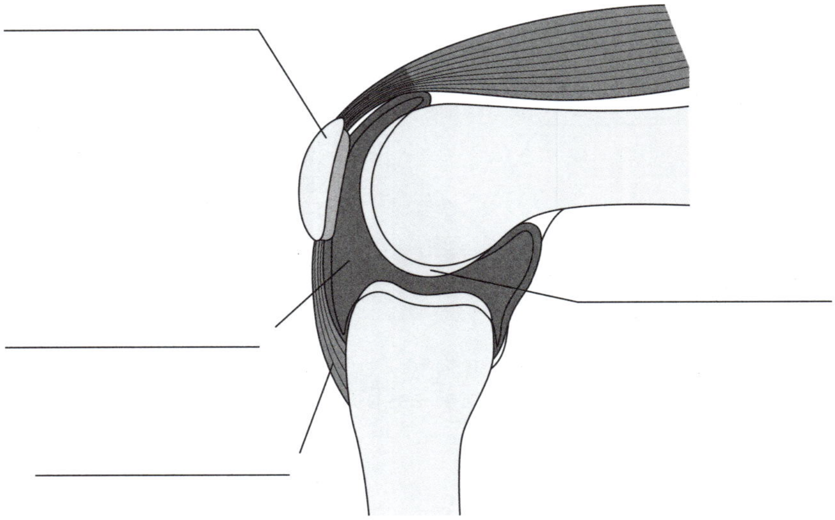

3 Match the structures in a joint with their function (job).

Structure
ligament
cartilage
fluid (liquid)

Function
keeps the joint slippery so bones do not rub together
joins two bones together
covers the end of the bone

2.4 Movement: muscles

Practical: Making a model arm

Learning objectives

- Describe the function of the major muscle groups
- Describe how muscles cause movement in the body
- Describe how antagonistic muscles control movement at a joint

Safety

- Be careful when making holes in the model arm.

Equipment and materials

- model arm template (cut-out)
- split pins
- string
- plasticine/cork
- coloured felt tip pens
- compass

Method

1 Photocopy page 44 and cut out both shapes on the template, along the solid lines.

2 Use a compass to make holes at the points marked '1', '2', and '*' on each shape, by pushing through the card onto a piece of plasticine or cork.

3 Join the pieces together by pushing a split pin through the '*' holes. Check the pieces move easily.

4 Cut two pieces of string 20 cm long.

5 Tie a knot in one end of each piece of string. Colour in around 2 cm of the string above the knot.

6 Push the string through hole 1 on the lower arm and then through hole 1 on the upper arm. Tie a second knot and again colour in 2 cm of string from the knot.

7 Repeat steps 5 and 6 but push your string through the holes numbered '2'.

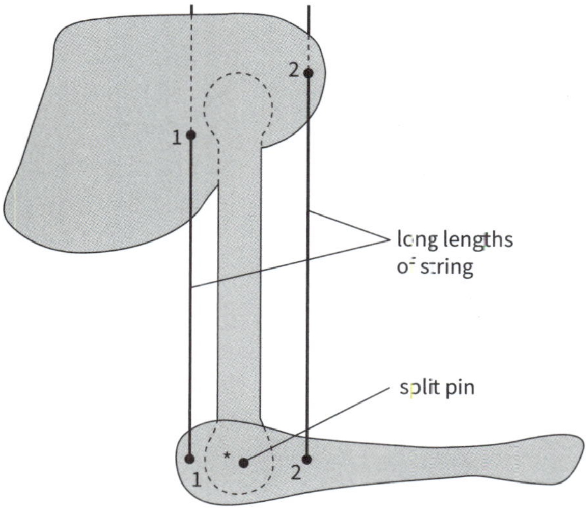

Model arm template

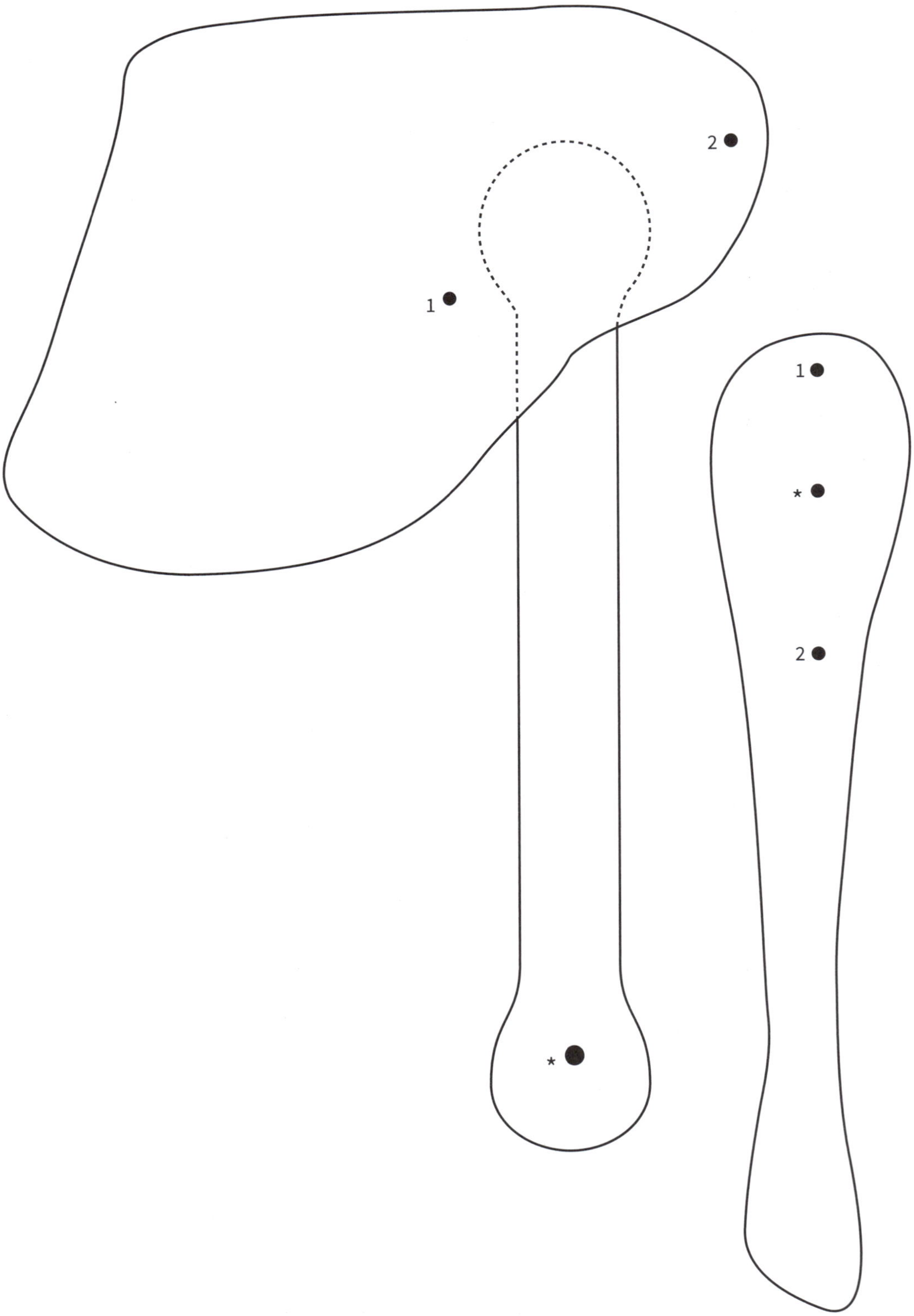

Questions

Use your model arm to answer the questions.

1 Complete the below table to show which parts of the body your model arm represents.

Part of the model	Structure represented
card	
	joint
string 1	
	biceps muscle
coloured section of string	

2 Describe how muscles cause movement.

____

____

3 Describe how antagonistic muscles control movement at a joint.

____

____

4 Complete the below table using the words *relaxed* and *contracted* (shorter).

Position of arm	Triceps muscle	Biceps muscle
straight		
bent		

BIOLOGY

Support

1 Use the words below to label your model arm.

muscle	bone	joint

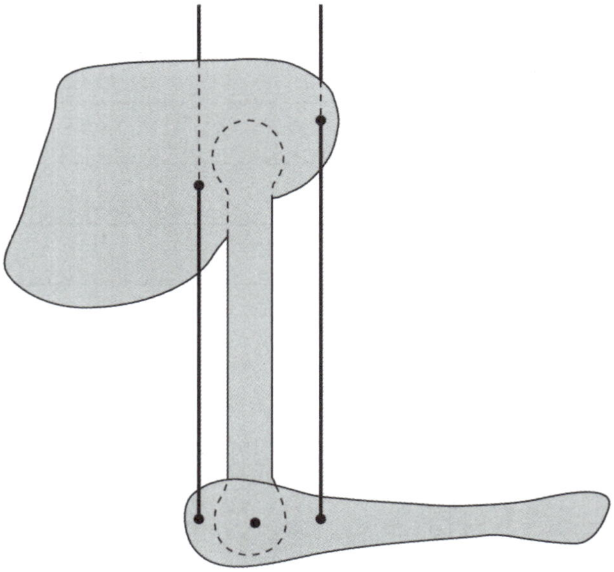

2 Complete the sentence to describe how muscles cause movement. Cross out the **two** incorrect words.
The muscle *contracts* / *relaxes*, *pushing* / *pulling* on a bone.

3 Complete the sentences to describe how antagonistic muscles control movement around a joint.
When one muscle contracts (gets shorter), the other muscle ______________ to cause movement.
To move in the opposite direction, the muscle that contracted must ______________, and the muscle that relaxed must ______________.

2.5 Breathing: lungs

Practical: Measuring lung volume

Learning objectives

- Describe the changes that happen when a person inhales and exhales
- Describe how a bell jar can be used to model breathing
- Describe a method used to measure lung volume

Safety

- Make sure you always use a clean or sterile mouthpiece.
- If you have breathing problems, such as asthma, you may wish to avoid measuring your own lung volume.

Equipment and materials

- 3-litre drinks bottle
- waterproof marker pens
- 500 cm^3 measuring cylinders
- rubber tubing
- large bowl or trough
- antiseptic cloths or disposable mouthpiece

Method

Calibrating (marking a scale on) a bottle

1. Fill a measuring cylinder to 500 cm^3 with water.
2. Pour the water into the drinks bottle, taking care it all goes in the bottle.
3. Mark the level of the water on the outside of the bottle.
4. Repeat the process, adding 500 cm^3 at a time, until the bottle is full.

Measuring your own lung volume

1. Half-fill a large bowl or trough (or sink) with water.
2. Place your hand over the end of the full drinks bottle to close it tightly. Carefully turn it upside down and place the neck of the bottle in the bowl of water.
3. Remove your hand, making sure that the neck of the bottle stays under the water.

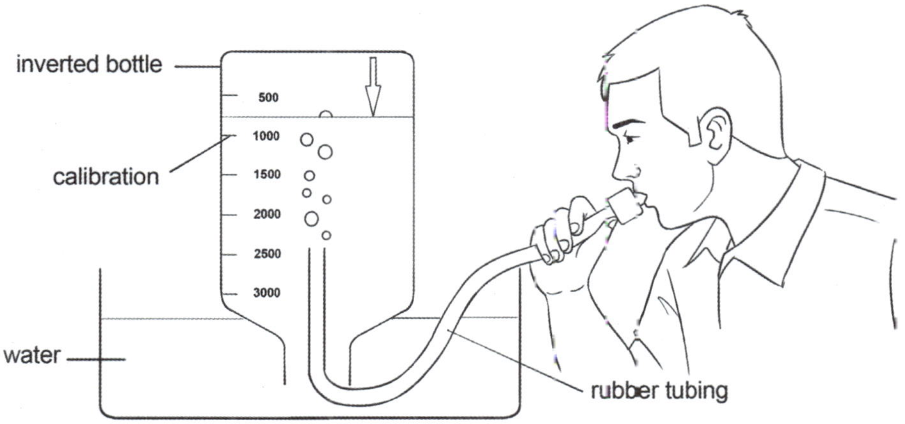

4 Take a length of rubber tubing and feed one end into the neck of the bottle.
5 Clean the other end of the rubber tubing with an antiseptic cloth.
6 Take a deep breath in. Then breathe out into the rubber tubing for as long as possible.
7 Record the volume of water displaced (moved out of the bottle). (This represents your lung volume.) To do this, read down the marker scale on the outside of the bottle until you reach the surface of the water.
8 Refill the bottle with water and repeat steps 2–7 for each member of your group.

Results

Lung volume = ______________________ cm^3

Questions

1 Calculate the total volume of air you exhaled in a minute, using the formula:
total volume exhaled (cm^3) = number of breaths (per minute) × lung volume (cm^3)

Total volume exhaled = ______________________ cm^3

2 Describe the main changes in your breathing system when you exhaled into the bottle.

____

____

____

Support

1 Calculate the total possible air breathed per minute using the below formula.

total possible air breathed per minute = breaths per minute × greatest volume of lung

Put your answers in the table.

Name	Breaths per minute	Greatest volume of lung in cm^3	Total possible air breathed per minute in cm^3
Student A	21	420	
Student B	19	510	
Student C	18	380	

2 Choose words from the list below to complete the paragraph to describe what happens when you exhale (breathe out).

up	down	in	out

The muscles between your ribs relax. This pulls your ribcage ______________________ and ______________________. The diaphragm relaxes, so it moves ______________________. Air is forced ______________________ of your lungs.

2.6 Breathing: gas exchange

Inhaled and exhaled air

Learning objectives

- Describe the process of gas exchange
- Describe how parts of the gas exchange system are adapted to their function
- Compare inhaled (breathed in) and exhaled (breathed out) air

Task 1

1 Label the diagram of the gas exchange system.

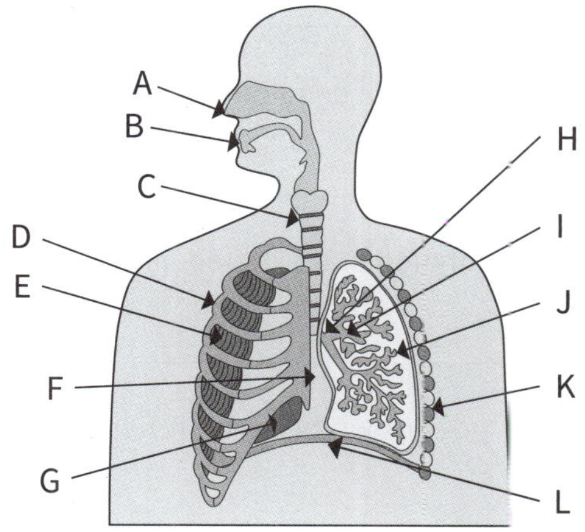

A ________________________ G ________________________

B ________________________ H ________________________

C ________________________ I ________________________

D ________________________ J ________________________

E ________________________ K ________________________

F ________________________ L ________________________

2 Describe how the ribs and alveoli are adapted to their function (job).

____

____

____

BIOLOGY

Task 2

Plot **two** bar charts: one to show the gases that make up inhaled air, and another to show the gases that make up exhaled air.

Gas	Inhaled air in %	Exhaled air in %
nitrogen	79	79
oxygen	21	16
carbon dioxide	0	5

(Figures rounded to the nearest whole per cent)

Questions

1 Name the structure through which gas exchange occurs in the lungs.

____

2 Name the gas that makes up the smallest part of exhaled air.

____

3 Name the gas that remains the same in inhaled and exhaled air.

____

4 Calculate the amount by which oxygen goes down between inhaled and exhaled air.

____

5 Describe what has happened to the oxygen that has been removed from the inhaled air.

____

6 A student states that 'the gas we breathe out is carbon dioxide'. Is this statement correct? Use the data in the table to help answer the question.

____

____

Support

1 Use the words below to label the diagram of the breathing system on page 49.

alveolus	bronchiole	bronchus	diaphragm
intercostal muscle	lung	rib	ribcage
nose	mouth	heart	trachea

2 This graph shows how you would plot a bar for how much nitrogen is found in inhaled air.

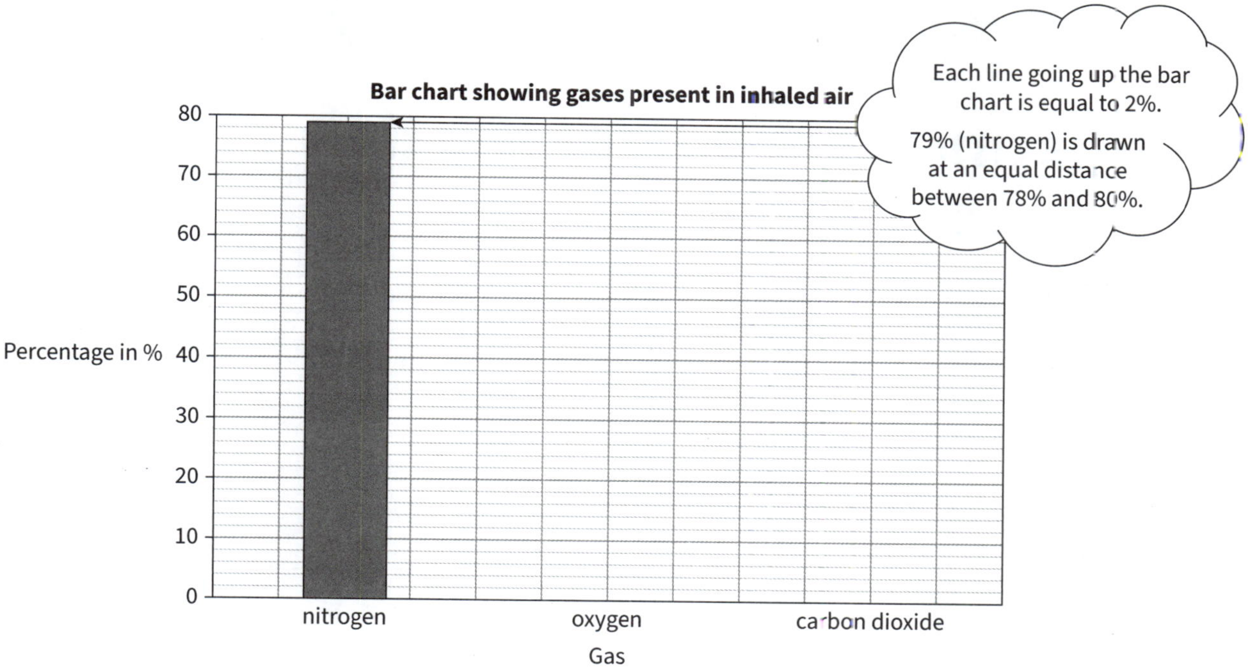

3 Now plot the bar for oxygen (21%) on the same axes.

2.7 Aerobic respiration

BIOLOGY

Investigating aerobic respiration

Learning objectives

- Describe the process of aerobic respiration
- Give the word equation for aerobic respiration
- Describe how the reactants and products of respiration move to and from cells

Task 1

1 Complete the word equation for aerobic respiration:

____________ + ____________ → ____________ + ____________ + ____________

(reactants) (products)

2 Complete the table to show how to test for the products of aerobic respiration.

Product	Chemical used	Positive result

Task 2

1 Choose words from the list below to complete the paragraph to describe what happens when you exhale (breathe out).

up	down	in	out

The muscles between your ribs relax. This pulls your ribcage ____________ and ____________. The diaphragm relaxes, so it moves ____________. Air is forced ____________ of your lungs.

Questions

1 State where in the cell aerobic respiration occurs. ________________________

2 Give the name of the blood part that transports glucose. ________________________

3 Describe how oxygen reaches the cell.

____

____

____

Support

Complete the sentences in the boxes to describe how the reactants of respiration reach the cell, and how the products leave the cell.

_____ is taken in when you breathe in. It diffuses into the blood in your _____.

_____ is carried by the _____ _____ cells. It then diffuses into the cell that needs it.

_____ dissolves in the _____ and is carried to the cell that needs it.

During digestion, carbohydrates are broken down into _____. This is absorbed (taken) into the blood in the _____ _____.

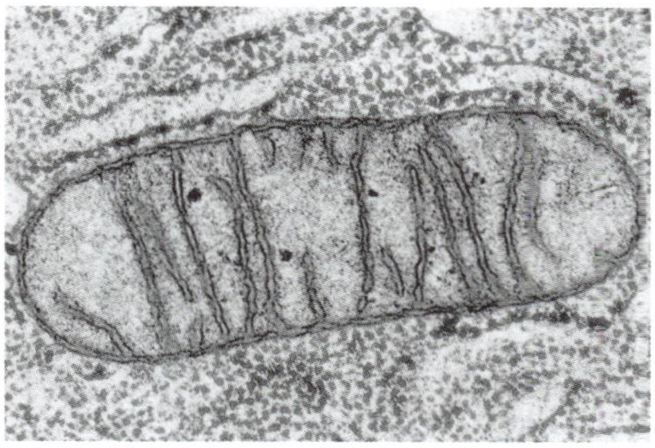

Respiration occurs inside the _____ within a cell.

The gas _____ _____ is produced. This dissolves in the blood _____.

It diffuses into the air sacs in the _____ and is released from the body when you breathe.

_____ is also produced by aerobic respiration.

2.8 Anaerobic respiration

Fermentation and food production

Learning objectives

- Compare the processes of aerobic and anaerobic respiration
- Give the word equation for anaerobic respiration
- Give the word equation for fermentation

Task

In this activity, you need to choose one food or drink product made using microorganisms. You will then use your research skills to find out how the product is made, before producing an information leaflet to explain the process to other students.

Your leaflet should:

- describe the type of microorganism involved in the production of the food or drink
- describe the importance of the fermentation reaction (include the word equation)
- include a step-by-step description of how the product is made on a large scale
- include pictures of any equipment used during production
- be made from one folded piece of A4 paper
- use correct scientific terminology, with any key words defined.

1 Choose a food or drink that is made using microorganisms: ______________________
Then research the following topics:
  - the microorganism involved in the making of your chosen product
  - how fermentation is used in the production process
  - how the product is made on a large scale.

2 Organize the production process into a step-by-step order. Find pictures to show the process.

3 Plan suitable subheadings to structure your leaflet and the key information you want to include.

4 Make your leaflet.

Questions

1 Complete the table to compare aerobic respiration, anaerobic respiration in animals, and fermentation by adding a tick (✓) in the column if the statement is true.

	Aerobic respiration	Anaerobic respiration	Fermentation
Glucose is a reactant.			
Oxygen is a reactant.			
Carbon dioxide is produced.			
Ethanol is produced.			
Lactic acid is produced.			
Water is produced.			

2 Write down the word equation for anaerobic respiration.

3 Give two reasons why animals normally respire aerobically.

Support

Summarize your research findings below.

Product:

Microorganism used:

Other ingredients needed:

Fermentation reaction:

How the product is made (step-by-step process):

Plan for layout of leaflet:

Key points

- Make sure your leaflet fits onto one folded piece of A4 paper.
- Include pictures of any equipment used during the production process.
- Use bullet points to summarize your main findings.
- Use scientific language, where necessary, but make sure you explain any key terms.

3.1 Nutrients

Healthy eating campaign

Learning objectives

- Define a balanced diet
- Name the seven parts of a balanced diet, giving examples
- Describe the role of each part of a balanced diet

Task 1

1 Find out about the parts of a balanced diet and their function in the body.
2 Summarize this information in the table below.
3 Add at least one example of a food product that is a good source of each part.

Part	Function(s) in the body	Example

Question

1 Describe the meaning of a balanced diet.

____

____

Task 2

In your group, plan and film a healthy eating YouTube / TV advertisement for the government. The advert should aim to encourage young people to eat a balanced diet. Your advert should last for no more than 2–3 minutes, and:

- include all seven parts of a healthy diet and explain their function
- give examples of foods that contain each nutrient
- encourage young people to eat a balanced diet.

Support

1 Draw a line to match each part of a balanced diet to its function (job) in the body.

Part		Function(s) in the body	
1	carbohydrates	A	needed in all cells and body fluids
2	lipids	B	keep you healthy
3	proteins	C	provide energy
4	vitamins	D	provides bulk (roughage) to food to keep it moving through the gut (your digestive system)
5	minerals	E	keep you healthy
6	water	F	growth and repair
7	fibre	G	provide energy / keep you warm / protect organs

2 Complete the definition below to describe the meaning of a balanced diet:

a diet that provides the right (correct) ____________________ in the right/correct ____________________

3.2 Digestive system

Model of the digestive system

Learning objectives

- Describe the process of digestion
- Describe the function of the main structures in the digestive system

Safety

- Take care when cutting wire – the ends can be sharp.
- Report any liquid spillages immediately to your teacher.

Equipment and materials

- plastic tubing
- modelling clay
- coloured card/paper
- large sheets of cardboard/card
- sticky notes
- sticky tape
- food dye/coloured liquid
- funnel
- wire and/or string
- scissors

Task

Work in a small group to produce a simple model of the human digestive system. On your model, add labels to identify the key structures and describe their functions. Once you have finished, you need to pour a coloured liquid through your model to show how food moves through the digestive system.

Plan

Look at the materials provided by your teacher and make a plan for building a model digestive system. In the space on the next page, draw a labelled diagram of what your model will look like.

1. Label each structure in the digestive system.
2. Describe the function of each structure. Add this information to the label.
3. Write down the materials you will use to make each part.

Evaluation

Models are never perfect. Evaluate how well your model represents the digestive system.

Positive features of the model	Negative features of the model

Support

1 Use the words below to label the diagram of the digestive system.

rectum	small intestine	stomach	large intestine	gullet	anus

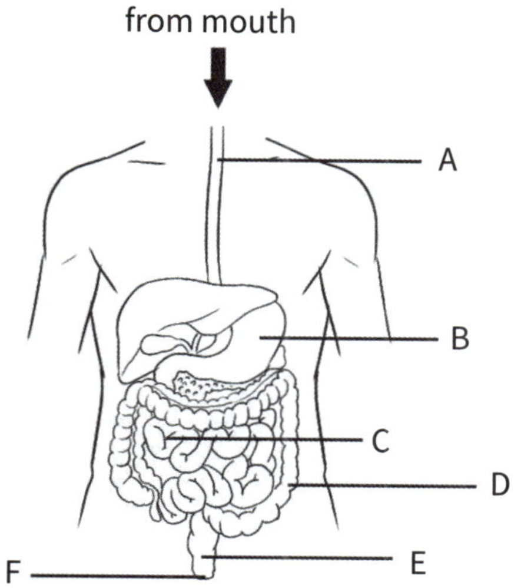

2 Write down the material that you will use to represent each organ in your model.

A: ______________________ D: ______________________

B: ______________________ E: ______________________

C: ______________________ F: ______________________

3 Draw a line to match each organ to its function (job).

Organ		Function	
1	rectum	A	food passes down this tube
2	gullet	B	faeces (waste) are stored here until they leave the body
3	stomach	C	water passes back into the body and faeces are formed
4	small intestine	D	small molecules of nutrients pass through the intestine wall into the blood
5	large intestine	E	food is mixed with digestive juices and acids

3.3 Food tests

Practical: Testing food solutions

Learning objectives

- Name the chemicals used to test foods for starch, lipids, sugar, and protein
- State the positive result for each food test
- Describe how to test foods for starch, lipids, sugar, and protein

Safety

- Wear safety glasses.
- Take care when using glass items, and when heating and boiling water.
- Avoid getting biuret solution, Benedict's solution, and iodine on your skin.
- Ethanol can easily catch fire. Keep away from flames.

Equipment and materials

- safety glasses
- boiling tubes
- boiling tube rack
- boiling tube holder
- dropping pipettes
- 250 ml beaker
- water bath (at 80–90 °C)
- food samples
- iodine solution
- Benedict's solution
- ethanol
- biuret solution
- 20 cm^3 measuring cylinder

Method

Making a food solution – to be used when testing for starch, sugar, fat, and protein.

1 Crush (break up) one type of food provided using a pestle and mortar.
2 Measure 20 cm^3 of distilled water using a measuring cylinder and add this to the crushed food.
3 Pour the solution made through filter paper placed in a funnel, into a boiling tube.

1: Testing for starch

1 Add 5 cm^3 of food solution to a boiling tube.
2 Add three drops of iodine solution to the boiling tube using a dropping pipette.
3 Shake the boiling tube gently and record your observations.
4 If starch is present, it will turn blue–black.

2: Testing for sugar

1 Add 5 cm^3 of food solution to a boiling tube.
2 Add about 1 cm^3 of Benedict's solution to the boiling tube (or more if the food has a strong colour) until the food solution looks blue.
3 Place in a water bath and leave for five minutes.
4 Remove the boiling tube from the water bath using a boiling tube holder. Place it in the boiling tube rack and record your observations.
5 If sugar is present, it will turn orange–red.

3: Testing for fat

1. Place a small sample of solid food (about 1 cm^3) into a boiling tube.
2. Measure 5 cm^3 of ethanol using a measuring cylinder and pour into the boiling tube.
3. Gently shake the tube and leave to stand for one minute.
4. Measure 5 cm^3 of water using a measuring cylinder and pour into a new boiling tube.
5. Pour the ethanol into the second boiling tube of water and record your observations.
6. If fat is present, it will turn cloudy.

4: Testing for protein

1. Add 5 cm^3 of food solution to a boiling tube.
2. Add three drops of biuret solution to the boiling tube using a dropping pipette.
3. Shake the boiling tube gently and record your observations.
4. If protein is present, it will turn purple.

Task

Summarize the tests in the table below.

Food group	Chemical	Positive result

Results

Record your observations in the table below.

Food tested	Starch present (✓)	Sugar present (✓)	Fat present (✓)	Protein present (✓)

Questions

1 Identify which of the foods you tested is a good source of protein.

---

2 Identify which of the foods you tested is a good source of starch.

---

3 Which of the foods tested should you only eat a little of in a balanced diet? Explain your answer.

BIOLOGY

Support

1 Add the colour you would expect to see for a positive result into the final column.

Food group	Chemical	Positive result

2 Use this table to record what you see.

Food tested	Observations (what you see)	Positive result (✓)
starch		
sugar		
fat		
protein		

3.4 Unhealthy diet

Energy requirements

Learning objectives

- Describe some health issues caused by an unhealthy diet
- State the meaning of a vitamin or mineral deficiency
- Compare the energy requirements of different people

Task

The graph shows the daily energy requirements (needs) of different types of people. Use the graph to answer the questions that follow.

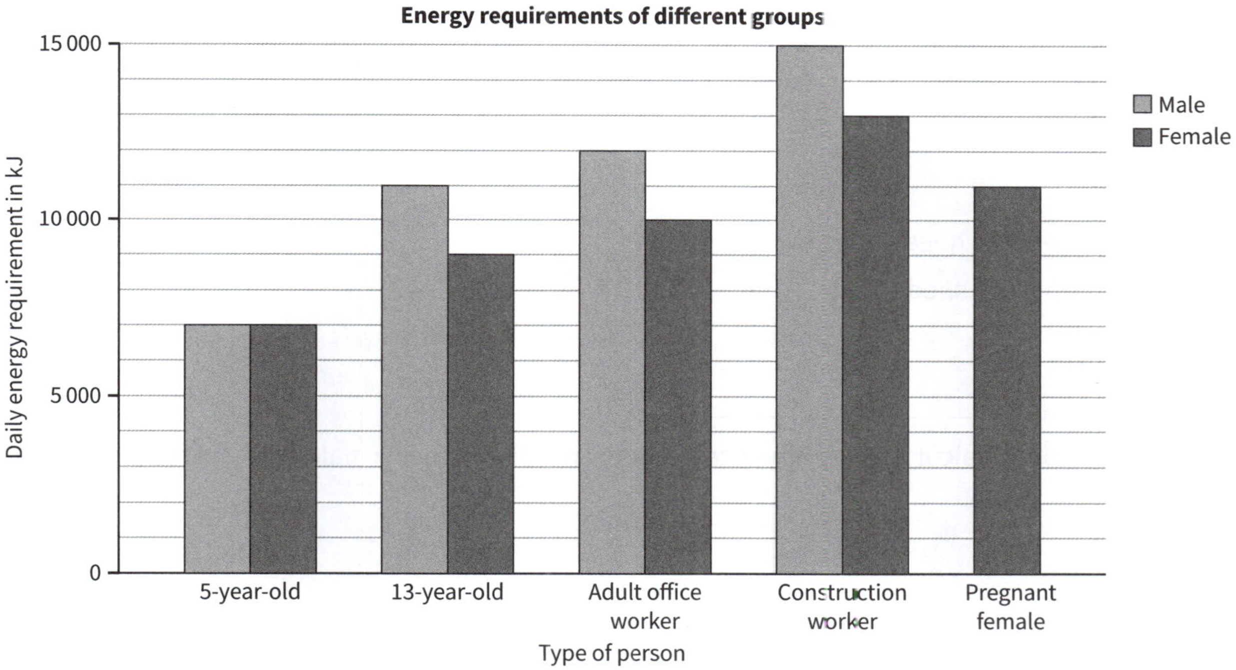

Questions

1 State which type of person on the graph has the highest energy need.

____

2 State the daily energy need of a 13-year-old girl.

____

3 Calculate the difference in energy needs between a male office worker and a female office worker.

4 Which statement about the data in the graph is true?

A Males require more energy per day than females at all ages.

B A pregnant woman requires more energy per day than a male office worker.

C As children grow, they require less energy per day.

D Female construction workers require more energy per day than male office workers.

5 Calculate the percentage increase in the energy needs of a boy between the ages of 5 years and 13 years.

Support

Use the graph to answer the question below.

1 Use the graph to find the needs of a:

male office worker = ____________________

female office worker = ____________________

Use this information to calculate the difference in energy needs between a male office worker and a female office worker.

3.5 Bacteria and enzymes in digestion

Practical: Investigating enzyme action

Learning objectives

- Describe the role of bacteria in digestion
- Describe the role of an enzyme
- Describe the role of enzymes in carbohydrate, protein, and lipid digestion

Safety

- Wash hands immediately if you get the enzyme or iodine solution on your skin.
- Wear safety glasses.

Equipment and materials

- safety glasses
- two boiling tubes
- boiling tube rack
- 10 cm^3 measuring cylinder
- two glass rods
- two pipettes
- spotting tiles
- stopwatch
- label pens
- iodine solution
- 1% starch solution
- 1% carbohydrase (diastase) solution
- distilled water

Task

- When starch is added to iodine, it turns a blue–black colour. You are going to add an enzyme (carbohydrase) to a starch solution (carbohydrate). You will then add the starch solution to iodine over time.
- Complete the hypothesis and prediction below, using the most appropriate words.

Hypothesis

When **an enzyme / a chemical** (carbohydrase) is added to **starch / sugar** (a carbohydrate), it will break the **starch / sugar** down. Eventually, it will be completely broken down into smaller parts. This is because **enzymes / chemicals** are biological catalysts. They **speed up / slow down** reactions without being used up.

Prediction

I am going to investigate this by adding **carbohydrase / iodine** to a starch solution. I will then add this to **carbohydrase / iodine** at different time intervals.
I predict that, over time, the starch and carbohydrase solution will **stop / keep** turning the iodine blue–black. This is because iodine is a test for **starch / sugar**, and the **carbohydrase / iodine** will have broken down the **starch / sugar**.

BIOLOGY

Method

1 Collect two spotting tiles.
2 Label one row on each spotting tile 'A' and another row 'B'.
3 Add a small drop of iodine in each well (small hole), using a dropping pipette.

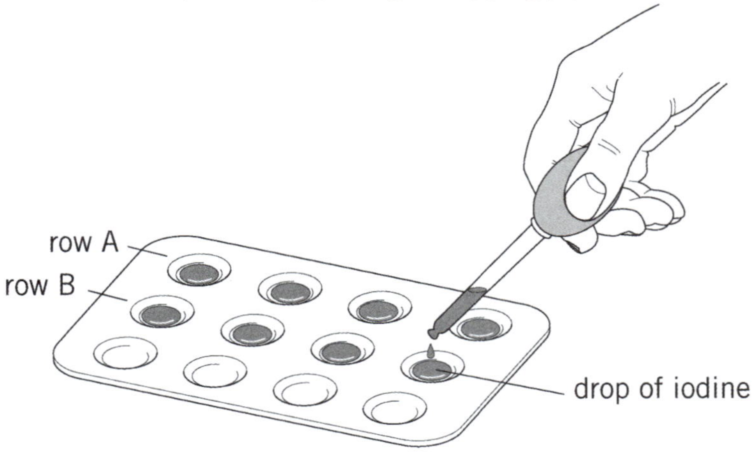

4 Collect two test tubes and label these 'A' and 'B'.
5 Measure out 5 cm^3 of starch solution using the measuring cylinder. Add to test tube A.
6 Measure out another 5 cm^3 of starch solution using the measuring cylinder. Add to test tube B.
7 Measure out 5 cm^3 of distilled water using a measuring cylinder and add to test tube A.
8 Mix the contents of test tube A (solution A) immediately using a glass rod (stirrer).
9 Measure out 5 cm^3 of 1% carbohydrase using a measuring cylinder. Add to test tube B.
10 Mix the contents of test tube B (solution B) immediately using a glass rod and start the stopwatch.
11 Using two clean dropping pipettes, add one drop of solution A into the first well on the spotting tile for row A, and one drop of solution B into the first well on the spotting tile for row B.
12 Continue adding one drop of solutions A and B from their separate test tubes into a new well of the spotting tile every minute.
13 Continue doing this until the colour stops changing for one of the solutions.
14 Record all your observations.

Results

Time in mins	Observations of colour change	
	Solution A (starch solution)	Solution B (starch solution and carbohydrase enzyme)

Questions

1 For solution A, describe your observations.

____

____

2 For solution B, describe your observations.

____

____

3 State how long it took for the starch to be broken down.

____

4 Do your results support your hypothesis and prediction? Explain your answer.

____

____

____

Support

In the table below, tick (✓) either 'orange' or 'blue–black' to show the colour you see at each minute interval for solution A and solution B.

Observations of colour change		**Time in min**								
		0	**1**	**2**	**3**	**4**	**5**	**6**	**7**	**8**
Solution A (starch solution)	**orange**									
	blue–black									
Solution B (starch solution and carbohydrase enzyme)	**orange**									
	blue–black									

The starch took ____________________ minutes to be broken down.
(*Tip*: Look for where the colour change stops.)

Conclusion

All of the results in row A showed a colour change from orange to blue–black. This is because

____________________ was present in all of these results.

In row B, there was no colour change after ____________________ minutes. This showed when the starch had been

digested into ____________________.

3.6 Harmful substances

BIOLOGY

Practical: Investigating harmful substances

Learning objectives

- Describe what a drug does and the difference between medicinal and illegal drugs
- Describe the dangers of smoking tobacco

Task 1: The harmful effects of smoking

Your teacher will demonstrate some of the effects of smoking on your body using a 'smoking machine'.

1 Complete the words to label the apparatus in the diagram below.

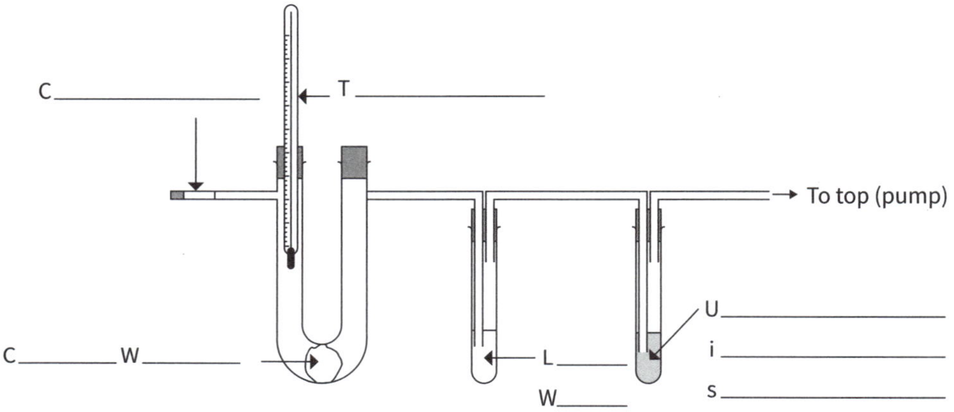

2 Add a description to explain what each piece of equipment is used for.

C: ____________________

T: ____________________

CW: ____________________

LW: ____________________

UiS: ____________________

3 Record your observations in the table below.

	Before	Fresh air	Cigarette smoke
Temperature in °C			
Colour of cotton wool			
Colour of universal indicator solution			
Colour of limewater			

Questions

1 State what was deposited (left behind) on the wool. ____________________

2 Describe the effect this chemical has on the body.

____

3 Describe what the colour change of the universal indicator solution shows.

____

4 Describe what the limewater shows. ____________________

5 Carbon monoxide is also present in tobacco smoke. Describe the effect that this chemical has on the body.

____

____

____

6 Another component of tobacco smoke is nicotine. Describe the effect that this chemical has on the body.

____

____

____

Task 2: Medicinal or illegal drug?

Produce a presentation about the difference between medicinal and illegal drugs in your country, and the effects they have on the body. Your presentation should be designed to educate other teenagers about the harmful effects of drugs (if used inappropriately and against a doctor's advice).

Support

Tick (✓) the box to show which description matches the harmful substance found in tobacco smoke.

	Carbon monoxide	Tar	Nicotine
a poisonous gas			
contains chemicals that cause cancer			
is a stimulant (speeds up activity)			
is a sticky, black material			
makes the heart beat faster			
stops blood cells carrying oxygen			
damages your lungs			
is addictive			

4.1 Photosynthesis

Practical: Testing a leaf for starch

Learning objectives

- Describe the process of photosynthesis
- Give the word equation for photosynthesis
- Describe how to test a leaf for starch

Safety

1 Avoid getting iodine on your skin.
2 Ethanol can easily catch fire. Keep away from a flame.
3 Keep long hair tied back and wear a lab coat and safety glasses.

Equipment and materials

- safety glasses
- Bunsen burner
- tripod
- gauze
- heatproof mat
- 250 cm^3 beaker
- boiling tube
- forceps
- white tile
- iodine
- ethanol
- leaf (that has been in sunlight for at least a day)
- dropping pipette

Method

1 Fill a 250 cm^3 beaker with 150 cm^3 of tap water.
2 Using a Bunsen burner, boil the water.
3 Use forceps to place the leaf in the beaker of boiling water. Leave it for two minutes.

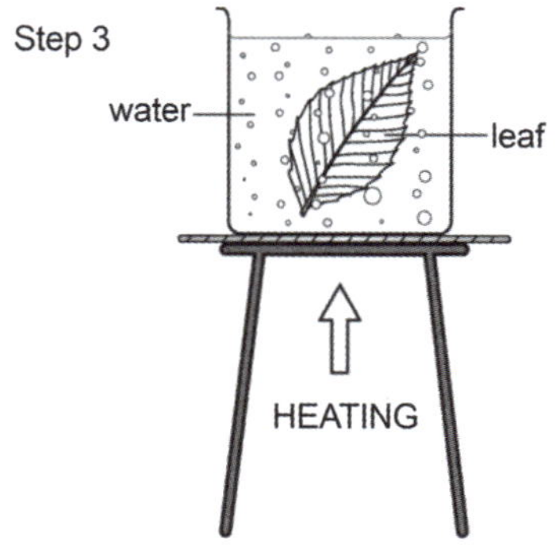

4 Turn off the Bunsen burner.
5 Add ethanol to a boiling tube. The ethanol needs to fill about a third of the boiling tube.
6 Remove the leaf from the water using forceps and place it in the boiling tube.
7 Put the boiling tube into the beaker of hot water.

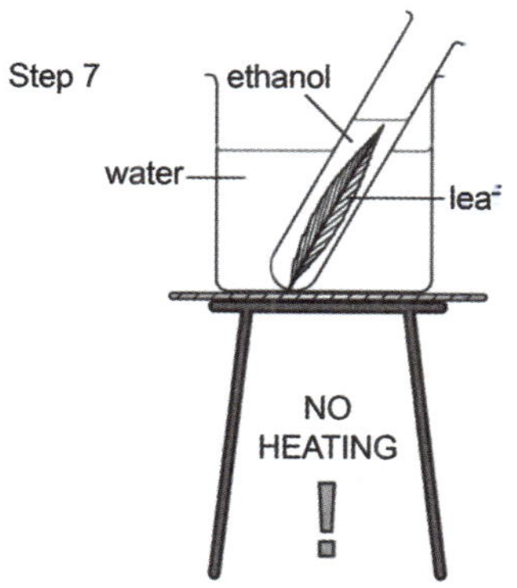

8 Leave for 15 minutes (or until most of the chlorophyll has been removed).
9 Remove the leaf from the ethanol using forceps and place into the beaker of water for 30 seconds.
10 Gently spread the leaf on a white tile using forceps.
11 Add iodine drops over the leaf using a dropping pipette.

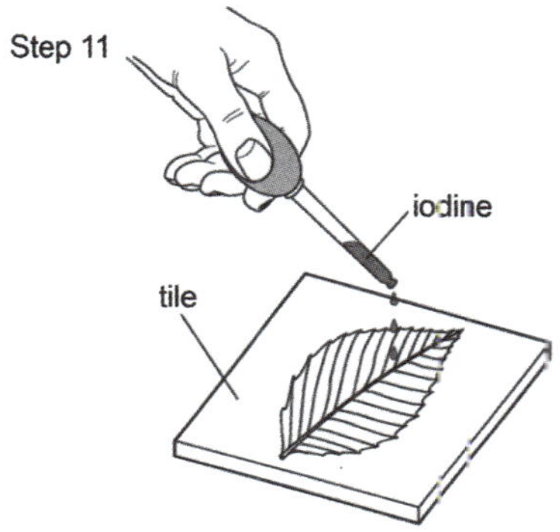

Risk assessment

Complete a risk assessment for this experiment in the table below.

Hazard/Risk	Safety measure taken to manage hazard/risk	Action needed in case of injury or contact with hazardous substance

Results

1 Describe your observations for this experiment.

2 Explain your observations.

3 Write down the word equation for photosynthesis.

BIOLOGY

Support

Risk assessment

Carefully consider all of the hazards (dangers) and risks in this experiment.

Complete the first table by using the correct information provided in the second table.

Hazard/Risk	Safety measure taken to manage hazard/risk	Action needed in case of injury or contact with hazardous substance

Hazard/Risk	Safety measure	Action
iodine (irritant)	tie long hair back	clean up any spills
Bunsen burner	keep away from open flames	wash off skin
ethanol (burns easily)	wear safety glasses	run cold water over burned skin

1 Describe your observations (what you saw) for this experiment.

____

____

2 Complete the word equation for photosynthesis:

carbon dioxide + ______________________ $\xrightarrow{\text{sunlight}}$ glucose + ______________________

4.2 Leaves

Practical: Observing stomata

Learning objectives

- Describe the main adaptations of a leaf
- Describe the role of stomata
- Describe how water travels through a plant

Safety

- Take care when using glass slides.
- Take care when lifting the microscope as it is heavy.

Equipment and materials

- microscope
- leaves
- clear nail varnish
- brush (to apply varnish to leaf)
- sticky tape
- microscope slide

Method

1. Paint a very thin layer of clear nail varnish over an area of about 1 cm^2 on the lower surface of the leaf.
2. Allow this to dry.
3. Take a piece of sticky tape about the same length as the glass microscope slide.
4. Press the tape over the lower surface of the leaf, with the dry nail varnish approximately in the centre.
5. Carefully pull the tape off the leaf. Make sure the nail varnish is stuck to the tape.
6. Stick the tape onto a clean glass microscope slide.
7. Observe the glass slide through the microscope. Record your observations.

Results

Draw a labelled diagram of your observations. Then add descriptions to say what each part does.

Questions

1 Name the substances that leave through the stomata.

2 Describe what this gas is used for in the leaf.

3 Name the substances that leave through the stomata.

4 Complete the table to describe the main adaptations of a leaf. The first one has been done for you.

Adaptation	Function
green	chlorophyll absorbs (takes in) sunlight
	allows gases to diffuse into and out of the leaf easily
large surface area	
	contain vessels to transport water and glucose
waxy layer	

Support

1 Label the diagram of the features of the lower surface of a leaf.

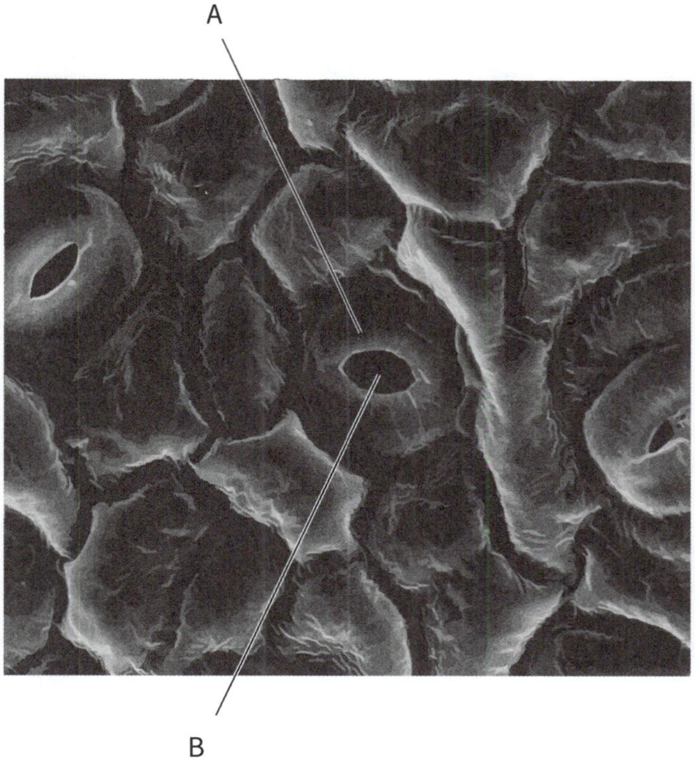

A ____

B ____

2 Complete the sentences to describe the function of these features.

Guard cells ____________ and ____________ the stomata. A single stomata is called a stoma.

When the stoma is open, ____________ diffuses into the leaf where it is used for photosynthesis.

____________ (produced by photosynthesis) and water vapour diffuse from the leaf, through the stomata, and out into the environment.

3 Draw a line to match each leaf adaptation to its function.

Adaptation	**Function**
1 green	**A** reduce water loss
2 thin	**B** allows gases to diffuse into and out of the leaf easily
3 large surface area	**C** contain vessels to transport water and glucose
4 veins	**D** chlorophyll absorbs (takes in) sunlight
5 waxy layer	**E** absorb (take in) as much light as possible

4.3 Plant minerals

BIOLOGY

Practical: Investigating fertilizers

Learning objectives

- Describe how a plant uses minerals for healthy growth
- Describe the symptoms of plant mineral deficiencies
- Explain why farmers use fertilizers

Safety

- Avoid getting fertilizer on your skin.

Equipment and materials

- two trays of six seedlings – one grown with fertilizer, one without
- balance
- ruler

Method

1 Decide which variable to record to compare the difference between seedlings' growth. Write this here:

____

2 Measure the variable for every seedling in the tray with fertilizer added. Record the results.
3 Now measure the variable for every seedling in the second tray, with no fertilizer added, and record the results.
4 For both conditions, record any seedlings that do not grow as a cross rather than a zero. These should not be included when calculating the mean growth.

Results

Design a suitable results table. Include a final column to calculate a mean for the variable you chose to measure.

Questions

1 Describe the difference between the two sets of seedlings.

____

____

2 Explain your answer.

____

____

3 Name the minerals present in the fertilizer you used.

____

4 Summarize the functions of different plant minerals and the symptoms of their deficiency (signs of a problem) in the table below.

Mineral	Function in plants	Symptoms of deficiency

Support

- You need to choose a variable to measure that will show you if the fertilizer has had an effect on the growth of the seedlings.
- Make sure you add your variable to your table in the space provided. Include the units used.
- To calculate the mean:
  - add up all your values
  - divide the total value by the number of values you had.

Experiment	Variable measured: Units:						
	1	2	3	4	5	6	Mean
Seedlings with fertilizer							
Seedlings without fertilizer							

Practical: Flower structure

Learning objectives

- Describe the function of the main structures in a flower
- Describe the process of pollination
- Compare the structure of wind-pollinated and insect-pollinated plants

Task 1: Flower dissection

Safety

- Tell your teacher if you have allergies to flowers or pollen.
- Take care when using sharp forceps.

Equipment and materials

- forceps
- flower
- hand lens
- sticky tape (optional)
- white tile (optional)

Method

1. Using forceps, carefully remove the sepals from the outside of the flower.
2. Draw a sepal in the results table. Record how many you found.
3. Repeat steps 1 and 2 for the petals, stamen, and carpel in turn.
4. Label the structures within a stamen and a carpel.

Flower structure	Sepal	Petal	Stamen	Carpel
Drawing				
How many?				

Questions

1 Complete the table to show the functions of the flower parts.

Part of the flower	Function (Job)
sepal	
petal	
filament	
anther	
stigma	
style	
ovary	

2 Describe the process of pollination.

____

____

Task 2: Pollination

Complete the table.

Structure	Insect-pollinated	Wind-pollinated
petal size		
petal colour		
nectar (sweet liquid) produced?		
pollen type		
amount of pollen produced		
attachment of anthers and stigmas		

BIOLOGY

Support

Task 1: Flower dissection

Follow the instructions on page 80 to dissect (cut up) a flower.

Questions

1 Using the diagram below match the correct letter to the parts of a flower.

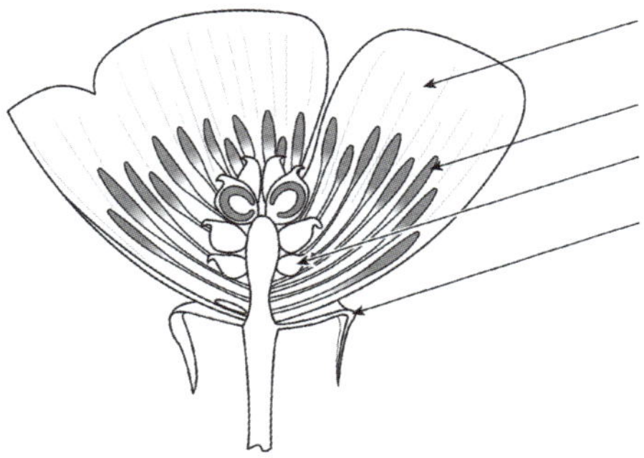

Flower part	Letter
1 carpel	A
2 petal	B
3 sepal	C
4 stamen	D

2 Tick the boxes to show which parts the carpel and the stamen contain.

Reproductive part	anther	filament	ovary	stigma	style
carpel (female)					
stamen (male)					

3 Name the cells produced by the anther. ______________________

4 Name the structure that pollen grains land on. ______________________

Task 2: Pollination

Circle the correct statement in each box to identify some features of an insect-pollinated plant and a wind-pollinated plant.

Structure	Insect-pollinated	Wind-pollinated
petal size	large / small	large / small
petal colour	green or brown / bright	green or brown / bright
nectar (sweet liquid) produced?	yes / no	yes / no
pollen type	sticky / low mass	sticky / low mass
amount of pollen produced	large amounts / small amounts	large amounts / small amounts
attachment of anthers and stigmas	loose, hang out of the flower / fixed, within the flower	loose, hang out of the flower / fixed, within the flower

4.5 Fertilization and germination

Practical: Seed formation

Learning objectives

- Describe the process of fertilization in plants
- Describe how seeds and fruits are formed
- Describe the main steps in germination

Safety

- Take care when using a scalpel because it is sharp.

Equipment and materials

- scalpel
- bean seed
- 5 beakers
- cling film
- 5 cotton wool pads
- cress seeds

Task 1: Seed formation

1 Cut your bean in half using the scalpel.
2 Draw your bean in the space below. Label the seed coat, embryo, and food store.

Questions

1 Complete the table to describe the function of each part of the seed.

Seed part	Function
seed coat	
embryo	
food store	

2 Name the part of a flower that develops into a fruit. ______________________

3 Name the part of a flower that develops into a seed. ______________________

4 Describe the main steps in fertilization.

___

___

___

Task 2: Investigating the effect of water on germination

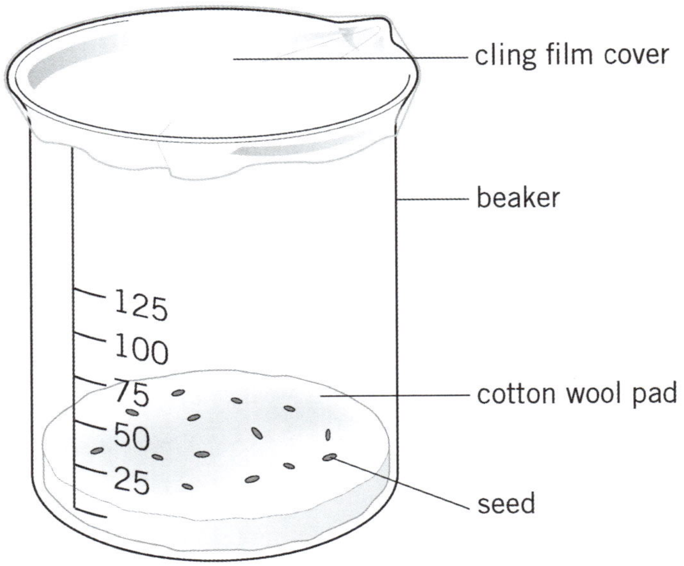

Five beakers have been set up to look at. The diagram above shows one example.

A different volume of water has been added to each beaker: 0 cm^3, 5 cm^3, 10 cm^3, 15 cm^3, and 20 cm^3.

In each beaker, 20 cress seeds have been placed on a cotton wool pad and left for a few days to germinate.

Results

1 Record the results of the practical in a suitable table.

2 Calculate the percentage of seeds that successfully germinated using the following formula:

$$\text{percentage germination} = \frac{\text{number of seeds germinated}}{20} \times 100 = \frac{\_\_\_\_}{20} \times 100 = \_\_\_\_\_\_\%$$

Questions

1 Describe the relationship you have recorded between volume of water and germination rates.

____

____

2 Describe the main steps in germination. ______________________________________

____

____

Support

Task 1

1 Draw a line to match each seed part to its function.

Seed part	**Function**
1 seed coat	**A** used by the plant until it can make its own food by photosynthesis
2 embryo	**B** cover on the outside to protect the seed
3 food store	**C** young root and shoot that will develop into the adult plant

2 Rearrange the steps to describe what happens during fertilization.

The pollen nucleus joins with the nucleus of the ovule.
The pollen nucleus travels down the tube.
The pollen grain lands on the stigma.
The pollen grain grows a tube down the style into the ovary.

Task 2

1 Record the results of the practical in the table below.

Volume of water in cm^3	Number of seeds germinated
0	
5	
10	
15	
20	

2 State which is the best volume of water for germination. ______________________

3 Choose the correct words to complete the sentences about the process of germination.

shoot	leaves	water	root	coat

The seed absorbs ______________, causing the seed ______________ to split. The ______________ grows down and the ______________ grows up. Finally, ______________ appear and the plant can start to make its own food.

4.6 Seed dispersal

Practical: Investigating seed dispersal

Learning objectives

- Describe the advantages of seed dispersal
- Explain how seeds are adapted for their method of dispersal
- Describe a method to investigate seed dispersal

Safety

- Take care when using scissors.

Equipment and materials

- metre rules
- scissors
- paperclips/sticky tack
- ‘helicopter seed’ template (cutout)
- large recording area (paper taped together)

Method

1 Photocopy the ‘helicopter seed’ template on page 87. Cut along the solid lines and fold along the dotted lines. Follow the diagram below. Add a small blob of sticky tack or a paperclip to the bottom folded area.

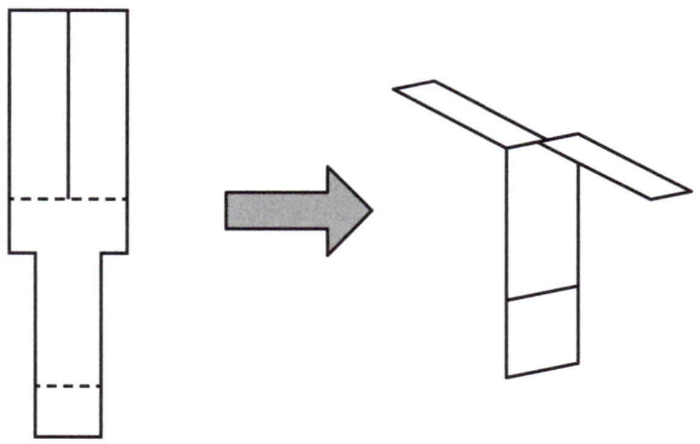

2 Drop the ‘helicopter seed’ from a height of 1 m above the central mark.
3 Measure the distance from the centre where it lands.
4 Repeat steps 2 and 3 three times.
5 Repeat steps 1–3 using a helicopter seed with different-length wings. (Make smaller ‘seeds’ by cutting the wings by 1 cm each time.)

Results

Complete the results table below.

Wing length in cm	**Distance from mark in cm**			
	Distance 1	**Distance 2**	**Distance 3**	**Mean in cm**

Calculate the mean for each wing length and add the value to your results table.

Questions

1 State the independent variable in your investigation. ______

2 State the dependent variable in your investigation. ______

3 Give **two** control variables in your investigation. ______

______

4 Identify the wing length that caused the seed to be dispersed the farthest. ______

5 Describe why seed dispersal is important for plants.

______

______

Helicopter seed template

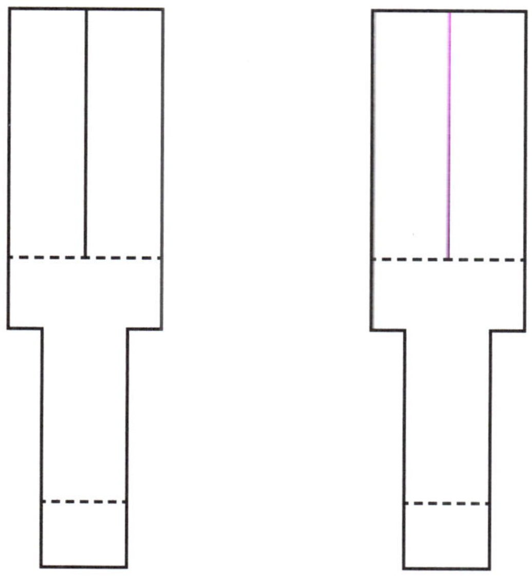

Support

Questions

1 Use the following variables to complete the sentences below:

wing size of the seeds   height the seed is dropped   distance the seed travels

The **independent** variable (factor you change) is ______________________________

The **dependent** variable (factor you measure) is ______________________________

The **control** variable (factor you keep the same) is ______________________________

2 Record your results in the table below.

Wing length in cm	Distance from mark in cm			
	Distance 1	Distance 2	Distance 3	Mean in cm
2				
4				
6				

3 Now calculate the mean for each row of distances. For each wing length:

a Add up the results for distances 1, 2, and 3.

b Divide your answer by 3 (because this is the number of distances you measured).

Add your mean values to your results table.

4 State which wing length caused the seed to travel the furthest. ______________ cm

1.1 The particle model

Factors affecting the properties of substances

Learning objectives

- Use the particle model to explain why different materials have different properties
- State the factors in the particle model that determine the properties of a substance

Task

1. Using the building blocks, create a model of a silver ring. Draw and label this in the space on page 90 and colour in the blocks.
2. Create a model of a gold ring. You should use blocks of a different colour to those you used for your silver ring. Draw and label this ring, and colour it in.
3. Write down why your silver ring would have different properties from those of your gold ring.

____

4. Create a model of an ice cube, draw and label this, and colour it in.
5. Create a model of a small pool of liquid water. You must decide which blocks to use and whether these should be different from those you used to model the ice cube. Draw and label this, and colour it in.
6. Write down why your ice cube would have different properties from those of your liquid water.

____

Questions

1. State the factors that affect the properties of substances.

____

____

____

2. Match the sentence starters to the sentence endings.

Sentence starters	Sentence endings
1 Materials are made of …	A … different particles.
2 In a substance, all the particles are …	B … particles.
3 Different substances are made of …	C … particles it is made from.
4 The properties of a substance are due to the …	D … the same.

3 A material is made of two types of particle. Explain whether or not the material is a substance.

____

____

____

Diagrams

Silver ring	Gold ring

Ice cube	Liquid water

Practical: Investigating the properties of matter

Learning objectives

- Compare the properties of a substance in its three states
- Describe the particles in the three states of matter
- Use the particle model to explain the properties of a substance in its three states

Safety

- Do not put any of the materials in your mouth.
- Wash your hands after holding the containers.
- Do not use too much force on the syringes.

Equipment and materials

Each group needs:

- five sealed (closed) syringes containing dyed (coloured) water, oil, air, sand, and small blocks of wood
- four sealed clear plastic bottles/containers containing dyed water, oil, air, and a block of wood

Method

1. Through the use of models and discussion, complete **Table 1** to describe the arrangement, distance apart, and movement of particles in the solid, liquid, and gas states.
2. You will then be given 2 minutes to look at substances in each of the solid, liquid, and gas states. Make a note of what you see in **Table 2** as you go.
3. Using the syringes and bottles containing the wood and sand, test to see if the substances in the solid state can be compressed (pressed into a smaller shape), flow, or take the shape of their container.
4. Repeat this with the syringes and bottles containing water and oil. Make a note of what you see.
5. Repeat this with the syringe and bottle containing air. Make a note of your observations (what you notice).

Results

Through the use of models and discussion, complete **Table 1** below:

	Solid state	Liquid state	Gas state
Particle diagrams			
Arrangement of particles			
Distance between particles			
Movement of particles			

Complete **Table 2** below with your observations of substances in the three states of matter:

State of matter	Solid	Liquid	Gas
Can you compress the substance?			
Does the substance flow?			
Does the substance take the shape of its container?			

Questions

1 Using **Table 1**, write a short paragraph describing the arrangement and movement of particles, and the distance between them, in each state of matter.

2 Give **two** differences and **one** similarity in the properties of a substance when it is in the solid and liquid states.

3 Compare how much substances in the liquid and gas states flow and can be compressed (pressed into a smaller shape).

4 Use the particle model to explain why:

a ice cannot be compressed (made smaller) in the solid state.

b water can flow in the liquid state.

c water vapour takes the shape of its container in the gas state.

Support

Complete **Table 1** on page 92. Describe the arrangement, distance apart, and movement of particles in the solid, liquid, and gas states. Use the suggestions given in the table below (not always in the correct order).

Arrangement	no pattern / no pattern / in a pattern
Distance apart	touching their neighbours / touching their neighbours / far apart
Movement	quickly and in every direction / vibrate (shake) on the spot / moving over each other in different directions

Complete **Table 2** on page 92. Use the suggestions given in the table below (not always in the correct order).

Can you compress (press) the substance (to make smaller) in this state?	yes, a lot / no / no
Does the substance in this state flow?	yes / yes / no
Does the substance in this state take the shape of its container?	no, its shape is fixed unless you apply a force / it takes the shape of the whole container / it takes the shape of the bottom of its container

Draw lines to match the state of water to its property, and then to the explanation of that property using the particle model.

State	Property	Explanation
Ice, water in the solid state, …	… cannot be compressed …	… because its particles move from place to place, in all directions, over each other.
Water in the liquid state …	… takes the shape of its container …	… because its particles spread out really far apart and move around in all directions.
Water vapour, water in the gas state, …	… can flow …	… because its particles are touching in a fixed position.

1.3 Density

Comparing densities

Learning objectives

- Define mass, volume, and density
- Explain why the same substance has different densities in each of its three states
- Explain why different substances in the solid state have different densities

Task

1. In groups of five to eight people, find some space and use tape to mark out a box on the floor measuring 1 m × 1 m.
2. Model the particles in a substance in the solid state. Arrange yourselves into a regular (fixed) arrangement inside the box (if you can, it does not matter if you are not all inside the box), making sure you are all touching shoulders and not moving off your spot.
3. Count the number of students standing inside the box.
4. Model the particles in a substance in the liquid state. Rearrange yourselves so you are in a loose arrangement (one that is not fixed), still touching shoulders, but gently moving around past one another.
5. Freeze and then count the number of students inside the box. Is it more, less, or the same as it was when you were forming a model of a solid?
6. Model the particles in a substance in the gas state. Spread out and move around in different directions.
7. Freeze and then count the number of students inside the box (there might not be anyone in the box). Is it more, less, or the same as it was when you were forming a model of a liquid?

Questions

1. Write the definitions of:

   a mass

   ____

   ____

   b volume

   ____

   ____

   c density

   ____

   ____

2 State the factor in the particle model that explains why aluminium in the solid state has a different density from that of iron in the solid state.

___

___

3 Explain why aluminium has a lower density than iron in the solid state.

___

___

4 State the factor in the particle model that explains why a substance's density is different in each of its three states of matter.

___

___

5 Explain why aluminium in the solid state has a higher density than aluminium in the liquid state.

___

___

6 Explain why aluminium in the liquid state has a higher density than aluminium in the gas state.

___

___

Support

1 Draw lines to match the key words *mass*, *volume*, and *density* to their definition.

mass	the amount of matter in an object
volume	the mass of a substance in a certain volume
density	the amount of space an object takes up

2 The properties of a substance depend on four things (or factors):

- what its particles are like, for example, their shape and size
- how its particles are arranged and separated (their distance apart)
- how its particles move
- how strongly its particles hold together.

From the list above, choose the factor that explains:

a why aluminium in the solid state has a different density to that of iron in the solid state.

b why a substance's density is different in each of its three states of matter.

1.4 Melting and freezing

Practical: Measuring the cooling of stearic acid

Learning objectives

- Describe what happens to the particles in a substance when it melts or freezes
- State the factor in the particle model that explains why different substances have different melting points

Safety

- The stearic acid and test tubes are very hot – take care when collecting them from the water bath and moving them around the classroom.
- Do not mix the solid or move the thermometer once the stearic acid has started freezing.

Equipment and materials

- one test tube of stearic acid, pre-heated
- one test tube holder/tongs
- one test tube rack
- one thermometer
- one stopwatch

Method

1 Place a thermometer into the stearic acid in the water bath. Measure and record the temperature. This is the temperature at $t = 0$.

2 Carefully collect a test tube from the water bath and immediately start the stopwatch (clock). Quickly and carefully take the test tube to your workstation and place it in a test tube rack.

3 Measure the temperature of the stearic acid every 30 seconds for 10 minutes, as directed by your teacher. Write down your results in the table below. Then plot those results on the graph.

Results

1 Complete the practical and fill in the table below.

Time in min	Temperature in °C	Time in min	Temperature in °C	Time in min	Temperature in °C
0.0		3.5		7.0	
0.5		4.0		7.5	
1.0		4.5		8.0	
1.5		5.0		8.5	
2.0		5.5		9.0	
2.5		6.0		9.5	
3.0		6.5		10.0	

2 Plot your points on the graph below.

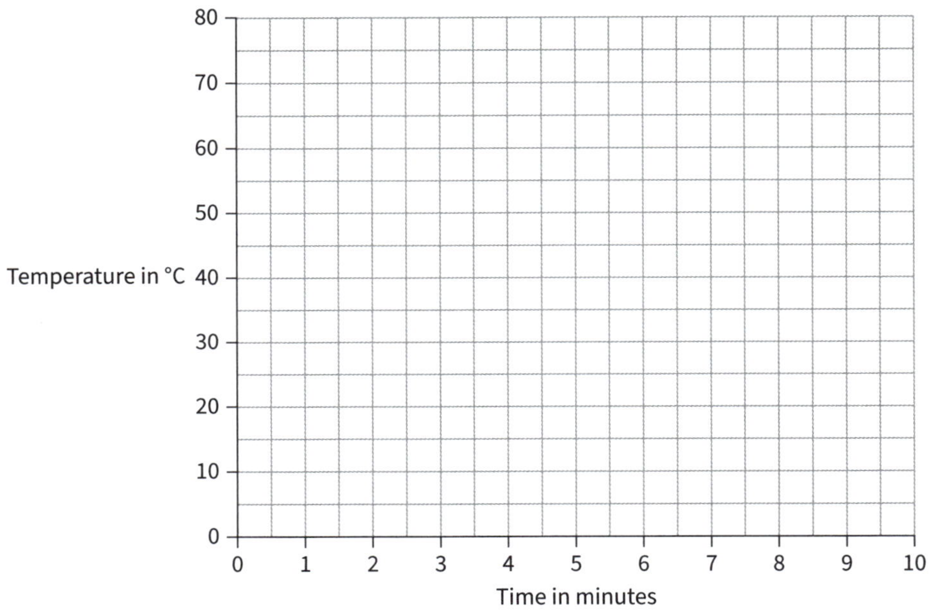

3 Label your graph with the states of stearic acid at each stage, and the melting point of stearic acid.

Questions

1 State the factor in the particle model that explains why different substances have different melting points.

____

____

2 Describe how the arrangement, movement, and separation (distance apart) of particles change when a substance melts.

____

____

____

____

The graph shows how the temperature of water changes with time as the water cools. It is a cooling curve.

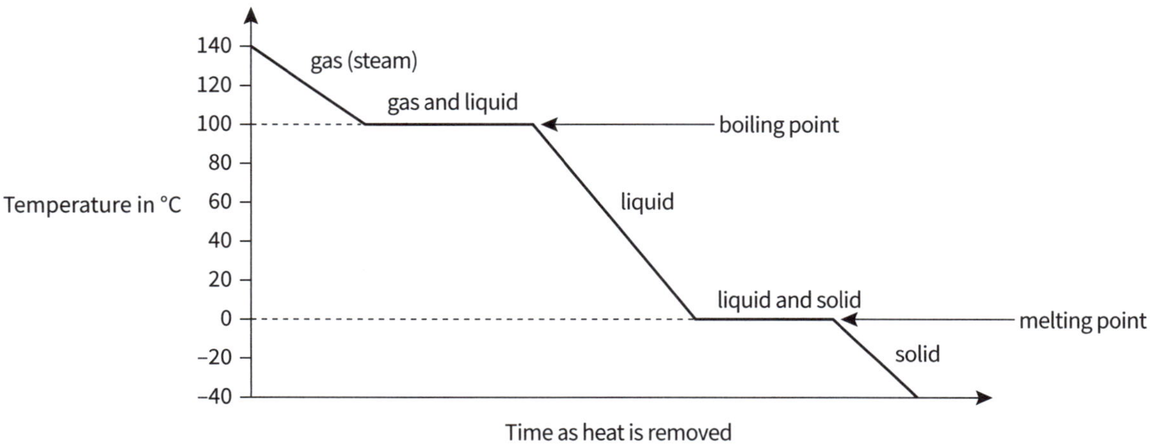

3 Describe the temperature–time graph for water.

____

____

____

____

4 Give the melting point of water from this cooling curve.

____

Support

These are factors in the particle model that explain why different substances have different properties:

- what its particles are like, for example, their shape and size
- how its particles are arranged and separated (their distance apart)
- how its particles move
- how strongly its particles hold together.

1 Below are descriptions of the arrangement and movement of particles in the solid and liquid states. Identify differences in the arrangement and movement of particles in the solid and liquid states.

Solids

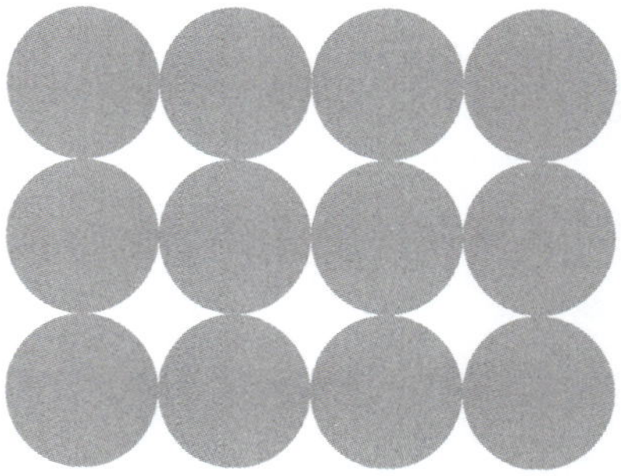

The particles are touching each other in a regular arrangement. They vibrate (shake) on the spot.

Liquids

The particles touch and move in all directions over each other. They do not form a regular arrangement.

2 In the following sentence, choose the correct **bold** words to describe how the arrangement, movement, and separation of particles change when a substance melts.

As a substance melts, the arrangement of its particles becomes **regular / irregular**. The particles start to move around **more / less** and **move past one another / vibrate (shake) on the spot**.

1.5 Boiling

Practical: Heating water

Learning objectives

- Describe what happens to the particles in a substance when it boils
- Predict the state of a substance at a given temperature from its melting and boiling points, where both are above 0 °C
- Give the boiling point of a substance from its temperature–time graph

Safety

- Safety glasses need to be worn at all times.
- The Bunsen burner, beaker, tripod, and gauze will all be very hot. Take care using them and only when told to by your teacher.
- Mix the water with the thermometer, but be careful as it might be hot!

Equipment and materials

- one 250 cm^3 beaker
- one thermometer
- one tripod
- one gauze
- one Bunsen burner
- one heat-proof mat
- one stopwatch
- one pair of safety glasses

Method

1 Measure approximately 200 cm^3 of water into a 250 cm^3 beaker.

2 Measure the temperature of the water using a thermometer.

3 Carefully light the Bunsen burner and heat the beaker of water on the blue/strong flame.

4 Measure and record the temperature of the water every minute until your water boils.

Results

1 Record the temperature of your water in the table below.

Time in min	Temperature in °C	Time in min	Temperature in °C
0		6	
1		7	
2		8	
3		9	
4		10	
5			

2 Plot these results on the graph paper.

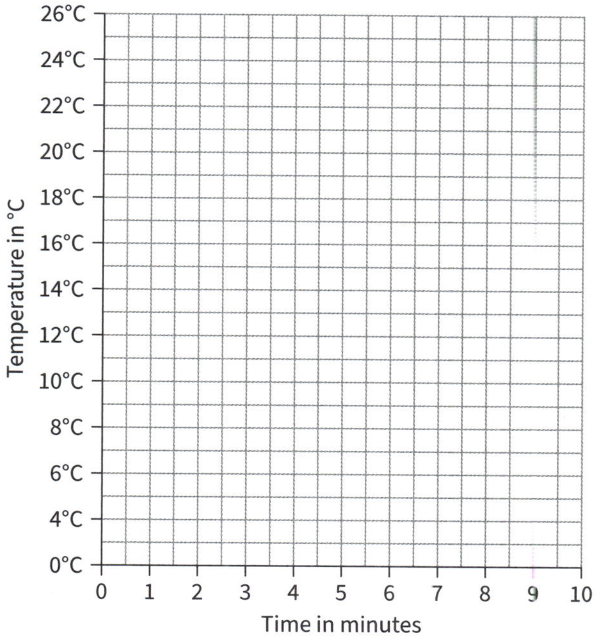

Questions

1 Describe the shape of the graph you have plotted.

____

____

2 State the temperature when the water began to boil. ____________°C

3 Describe how the boiling point of a substance can be identified from a heating curve.

____

____

4 Give the before and after states of a substance when it boils.

____

5 The melting point of gold is 1063 °C and the boiling point of gold is 2966 °C.

a Predict its state at 500 °C. ____________

b Predict its state at 3000 °C. ____________

6 Draw particle diagrams for a substance **before** and **after** it has boiled.

7 Describe how the particle arrangement, separation (distance apart), and movement change as a substance boils.

____

____

Support

These are factors in the particle model that explain why different substances have different properties:

- what its particles are like, for example, their shape and size
- how its particles are arranged and separated (their distance apart)
- how its particles move
- how strongly its particles hold together.

The melting point of gold is 1063 °C and the boiling point of gold is 2966 °C.

a Label the melting and boiling points of gold on the temperature scale below.

b Use this to predict its state at 500 °C and at 3000 °C.

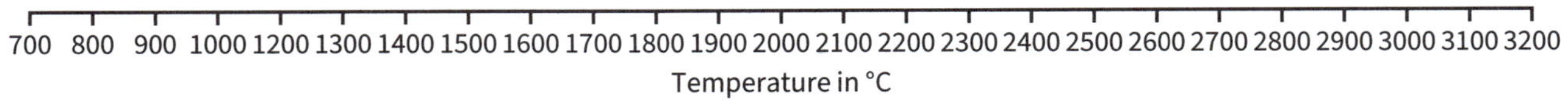

1.6 More changes of state

Practical: Recording evaporation

Learning objectives

- Compare the before and after states of evaporating, condensing, and subliming
- Describe what happens to the particles in a substance when it evaporates, condenses, and sublimes
- Compare what happens to the particles in a substance when it evaporates and boils

Safety

- Alcohol-based products can easily catch fire. Keep them away from all flames.

Equipment and materials

- one white tile
- two dropping pipettes
- one permanent marker pen
- dyed/coloured water
- dyed/coloured alcohol hand gel

Method

1 Draw two small, 5 pence-sized, circles on your white tile using a permanent marker pen. Label one as alcohol and the other as water.

2 Using the dropping pipettes, put one drop of alcohol hand gel into the alcohol circle, and one drop of water into the water circle. The alcohol hand gel may rub away the marker so be careful!

3 Leave your white tile flat on a windowsill.

4 Answer the questions below.

5 Return to your white tile and check if the amounts of alcohol hand gel or water have decreased. Make a note of which seems to have decreased more.

Results

1 Does it look like the amount of alcohol hand gel has decreased?

____

2 Does it look like the amount of water has decreased?

____

3 Which liquid seems to have decreased more?

____

Questions

1 Give the **before** and **after** states in the following changes of state:

a Evaporating ____________________

b Condensing ____________________

c Subliming ____________________

2 Describe how the arrangement, separation (distance apart), and movement of the particles change when:

a alcohol hand gel evaporates.

____

____

b water condenses.

____

____

c carbon dioxide sublimes.

____

____

3 Create a Venn diagram to show what is similar and what is different about evaporating and boiling.

4 Compare the changes in the arrangement, separation (distance apart), and movement of the particles in evaporating and boiling.

____

____

____

Support

1 Give the before and after states in evaporating, condensing, and subliming. Choose from the following pairs of states.

a solid → gas

b gas → liquid

c liquid → gas

2 Look at your descriptions from Question **2** on page 104.

Do you notice any similarities or differences between evaporating and boiling?

Write down when evaporating and boiling take place, and where in a substance they take place.

Use your descriptions and notes to create a Venn diagram in Question **3**.

Use your Venn diagram in Question **3** to compare the changes that take place during evaporation and boiling. Complete the comparison in Question **4**.

Practical: How does temperature affect the rate of diffusion?

Learning objectives

- Describe how the movement of the particles changes when a substance diffuses
- Use the particle model to explain how temperature, particle size, and state affect how quickly diffusion happens
- Use the particle model to explain what you see in a diffusion experiment

Safety

- Take care when using glassware. Ask an adult to clear away any broken beakers.
- Do not carry the beaker of hot water as it will be too hot to touch.
- Be gentle when placing the tea bags in the beakers to avoid spilling any hot water.
- Do not drink the tea.

Equipment and materials

- two 250 cm^3 beakers
- two tea bags
- one stopwatch

Method

1 Fill one beaker with 250 cm^3 of cold water.

2 Ask a teacher/adult to fill the second beaker with 250 cm^3 of hot water.

3 At the same time, gently place one tea bag in each beaker and start the stopwatch. Do not touch the beakers.

4 Every minute, look at the beakers. Make a note if you can see diffusion taking place, and how far the tea particles have diffused.

5 If your tea has diffused throughout the whole of the water, make a note of the time it took.

Results

1 Record what you saw in your beakers of cold and hot water in the table below.

Time in min	Description of beaker of cold water	Description of beaker of hot water
0		
1		
2		
3		
4		
5		
6		
7		
8		
9		
10		

2 Which beaker gave the faster time for the tea to diffuse? ______________________

Questions

1 Did diffusion happen faster at the higher or lower temperature? ______________________

2 Why do we need to keep the beakers still once the experiment has started?

____

3 Describe how the separation (distance apart) of tea particles changed when the tea diffused.

____

4 Use the particle model to explain how the following factors affect how quickly diffusion happens:

a temperature ______________________

____

b particle size ______________________

____

c state ______________________

____

5 Use the particle model to explain your answer to Question **4b**.

____

____

Support

Here are some factors that could affect how quickly diffusion occurs. Decide which factor is correct. Use this to help you answer the questions on pages 107–108.

- what its particles are like, for example, their shape and size
- how its particles are arranged and separated (their distance apart)
- how its particles move
- how strongly its particles hold together

Here are some images of the particle model:

a solid

a liquid

a gas

2.1 Elements

Researching the elements

Learning objectives

- Define an element and list some examples of elements
- Describe what the Periodic Table shows and use it to find a named element

Task

1 Using the resources given to you by your teacher, you are going to research an element and create an information poster or leaflet about your element.
2 Find the name of your chemical element and its chemical symbol from the Periodic Table. Write these in big letters in the middle of your poster or on the front of your leaflet.
3 Use the resources to find out information about your element.
4 On your poster or leaflet, you should include answers to the following questions:
   - Where is the element found?
   - When and how was the element discovered?
   - What is the element used for?
   - What properties does the element have?
   - How do the element's properties make it suitable for the uses you have found out about?
   - Are there any interesting or unusual facts about the element? (e.g. If the element is not found naturally, why? Is the element hazardous? Where does its name come from?)

Questions

1 State what the Periodic Table shows.

____

2 State how the elements are grouped in the Periodic Table.

____

3 Write down the definition of the key word *element*.

____

4 Use the Periodic Table to write down the chemical symbols for these lists of elements. Each list should spell a word.

a carbon hydrogen iodine phosphorus sulfur _______________

b fluorine lithium carbon potassium _______________

c sulfur hydrogen iodine phosphorus _______________

d phosphorus hydrogen yttrium silicon caesium _______________

e barium sodium sodium _______________

f sulfur lithium nitrogen potassium yttrium ______

g scandium argon erbium ______

h germanium nickel uranium sulfur ______

i dysprosium nitrogen americium iodine tellurium ______

j helium lithium cobalt platinum erbium ______

5 Use the Periodic Table to write down the names of each of the elements used to spell the words below.

a P I Ra Te ______

b Mo U Se ______

c Lu C K Y ______

d F La S H ______

e V I O Li N ______

6 Write your own words using only symbols from the Periodic Table. Write down the names of those elements in order and give them to a partner to decipher (work out).

Support

1 In the following sentence, choose the correct **bold** word to give the meaning of the key word *element*.

An element is a substance that **can** / **cannot** be broken down into other substances.

2 Match the sentence starter to the correct ending to describe what the Periodic Table shows and how it is arranged.

Sentence starter	Possible sentence endings
	… lots of different gases, grouped in alphabetical order.
The Periodic Table shows …	… all the known elements, grouped together with elements with similar properties.
	… some of the chemicals found on Earth, grouped together in no particular order.

3 Match the element names to their correct chemical symbol. Use the Periodic Table to help you. You can then use this information to answer Questions **4** and **5** on pages 109–110.

helium	H
lithium	Se
carbon	Li
nitrogen	Na
oxygen	O
fluorine	F
sodium	Ni
silicon	Co
phosphorus	K
sulfur	Si
argon	Pt
potassium	P
scandium	Cs
vanadium	U
cobalt	S
nickel	N
germanium	Mo
selenium	C
yttrium	I
molybdenum	Ge
tellurium	Am
iodine	Y
caesium	Sc
barium	Ba
lanthanum	La
platinum	Ar
dysprosium	Er
erbium	Dy
uranium	V
americium	Te

2.2 Atoms

Properties of atoms and elements

Learning objectives

- Define an atom
- Define an element in terms of its atoms

Task

1 Choose the correct words from the box below to complete the paragraph about atoms.

the same	different	colour	element	properties

Atoms are the smallest parts of an ______________________ that can exist. All atoms in an element are ______________________, but atoms from different elements are ______________________ from one another. When atoms are on their own, they do not have the same ______________________ as the element. When there is a group of many atoms together, they have the same properties as the element, for example, ______________________.

2 Match the pictures to the correct labels.

a **b** **c** **d**

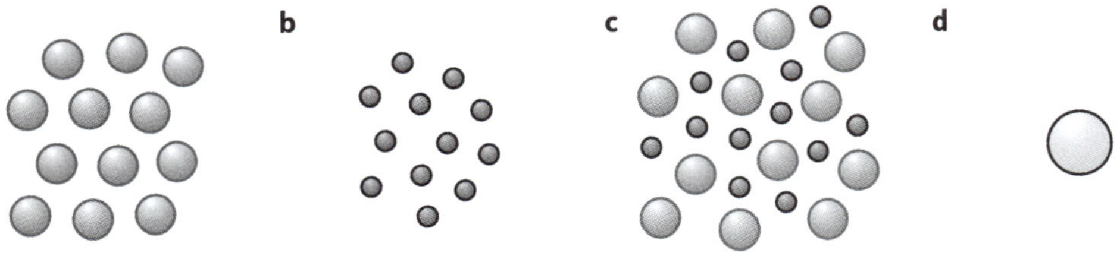

lots of atoms from two different elements	several atoms from one element only	an individual atom	several atoms from one element only

3 Atoms of hydrogen are smaller than atoms of iron. Which diagram in Question **2** above represents hydrogen atoms and which diagram represents iron? How did you decide?

____

____

____

4 Write a story about an atom that gets separated from its 'element family', and the changes in properties it experiences because of this.

You may want to use words from the list below.

physical	properties	the same	different	colour	chemical

Questions

1 How many elements are there in a piece of gold?

2 Jewellery is sometimes made of white gold, which often contains gold and silver. How many elements are there in white gold?

3 Iron is very good at conducting heat. Would one iron atom be able to conduct heat?

4 If a silver ring weighing 10 g has 60 000 000 000 000 000 000 000 atoms in it, how many atoms does a block of silver weighing 100 g have in it?

Practical: Introducing compounds

Learning objectives

- Define a compound
- Explain whether a molecule diagram shows an element or a compound
- Explain why a compound has different properties to the elements whose atoms are in the compound

Safety

- Wear safety glasses throughout the practical.
- Do not use electrical equipment near water.
- Take care when using glass items.
- Do not breathe in iron filings.

Equipment and materials

- one battery pack
- three wires
- one light bulb
- two crocodile clips
- three watch glasses
- one bar magnet
- three test tubes
- one test tube rack
- some iron filings
- some sulfur (roll)
- some iron sulfide
- one spatula

Method

1 Place a small amount of iron, sulfur, and iron sulfide onto three separate, clean watch glasses.

2 Use the following circuit to test if each substance allows the bulb to light. Record what you observe in the table (see Results section).

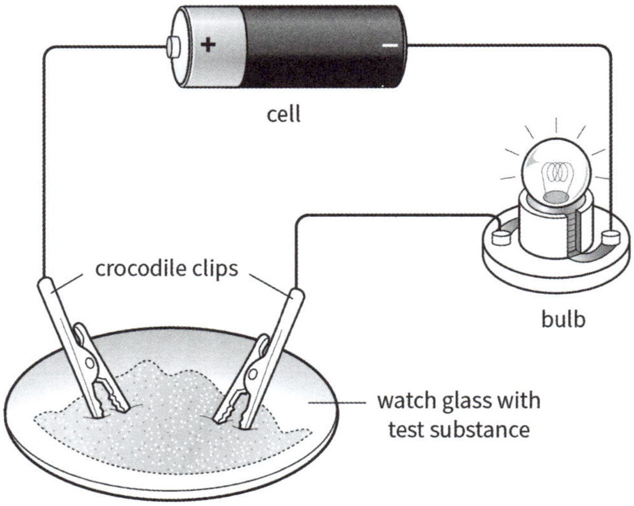

3 Place a small amount of each substance into three clean test tubes (one substance per test tube). Run a bar magnet along the sides of each test tube to see if any of the substances are attracted to the magnet. Record what you observe in the table.

4 Look at the substances and think about what state you think each substance is in. Record what you observe in the table.

Results

Observations	Iron	Sulfur	Iron sulfide
Does the bulb light?			
Is it attracted to the bar magnet?			
What does the substance look like?			
What state is the substance in?			

Questions

1 Write down the definition of a compound.

2 Describe how the properties of iron are different from those of iron sulfide.

3 Explain why iron sulfide has different properties from those of iron.

4 Determine and explain which of diagrams A–C show(s) an element and which show(s) a compound.

A

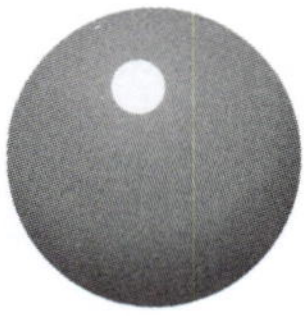

B

C

Support

1 Match the sentence starter to the correct ending to make the definition of a compound.

Sentence starter	Sentence endings
A compound is a substance that …	… is in the liquid state at room temperature. … is only made up of one type of atom. … is made up of atoms of two or more elements, strongly joined together.

2 Choose the correct words in **bold** to complete the sentence below. The sentence explains why iron sulfide has different properties from those of iron.

Iron sulfide particles are **the same as** / **different from** iron particles.

3 Match the explanations below to the particle diagram(s) on page 115.

- This diagram shows a compound because it is made up of atoms of two elements.
- This diagram shows an element because it has atoms of only one type.

2.4 Chemical formulae

Naming compounds and chemical formulae

Learning objectives

- Name a familiar two-element compound
- Determine the chemical formula of a compound, given the relative numbers of atoms of the elements in the compound
- Determine the chemical formula of a compound, given a labelled molecule diagram

Task

1 As a class, decide what colour block will represent each of the following elements:
  - **a** carbon, C
  - **b** hydrogen, H
  - **c** oxygen, O
  - **d** sulfur, S

2 Create a model of a particle of CO using your building blocks. Connect one block of your carbon colour to one block of your oxygen colour.

3 Create a model of a particle of CO_2 using your building blocks. Think carefully about how many blocks of your carbon colour and how many blocks of your oxygen colour you will need.

4 Create models of H_2O, SO_2, SO_3, and O_2 particles using the correct number of blocks to represent each element.

5 Draw these models below, and label and colour each different element.

6 Using the naming rules discussed as a class, name each of the compounds you have drawn.

CHEMISTRY

Questions

1 Match the compound names to their correct description.

1 sulfur dioxide	**A** one carbon atom and one oxygen atom
2 sulfur monoxide	**B** one carbon atom and two oxygen atoms
3 carbon monoxide	**C** one sulfur atom and two oxygen atoms
4 carbon dioxide	**D** one sulfur atom and one oxygen atom

2 Give the number and types of atom in a particle of:

a water, H_2O ____________________

b chlorine, Cl_2 ____________________

c sodium chloride, NaCl ____________________

d ammonia, NH_3 ____________________

3 Name the particles shown in the following labelled molecule diagrams.

a

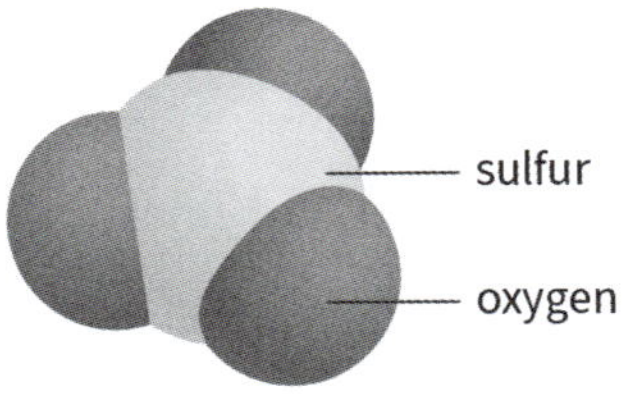

____

b

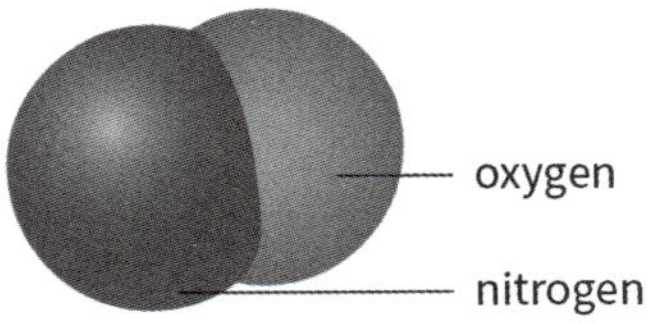

____

4 Write the chemical formulae for the particles shown in the following labelled molecule diagrams.

a

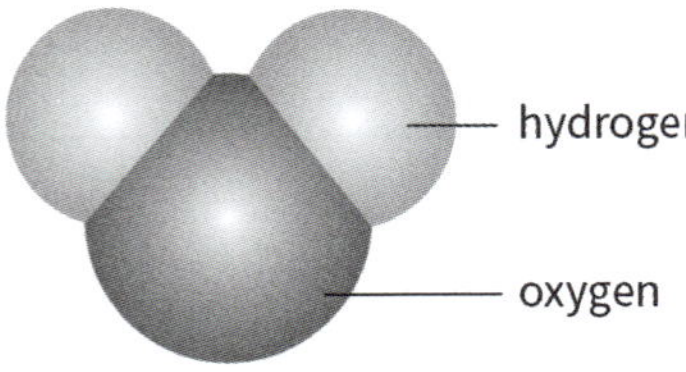

____

b

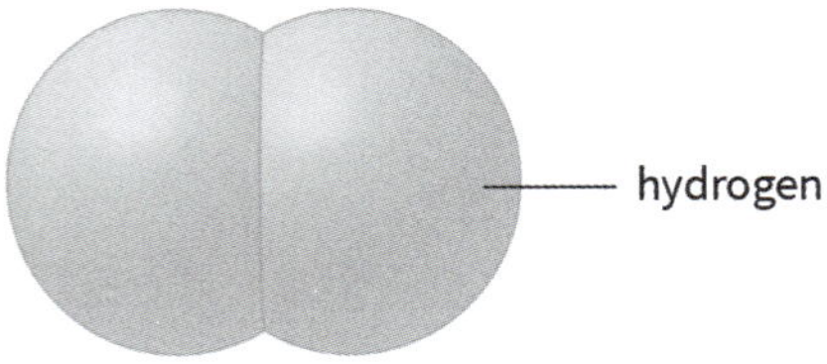

____

c

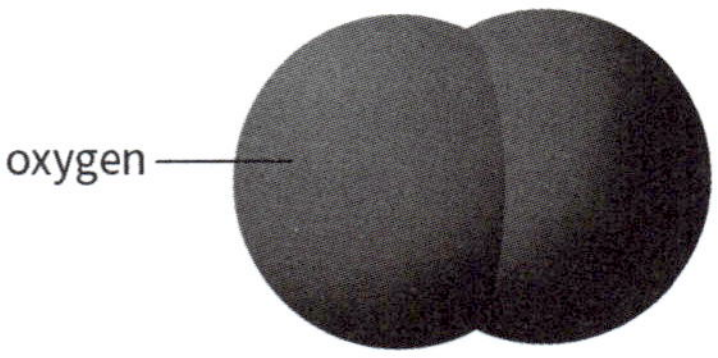

____

5 Write the chemical formula of the compound that is made up of one zinc atom to one oxygen atom.

____

6 Write the chemical formula of the compound that is made up of one sulfur atom to three oxygen atoms.

____

Support

1 Draw lines to match the formulae to the correct descriptions of the relative numbers of atoms of each element.

H_2O	one nitrogen atom with three hydrogen atoms
Cl_2	two chlorine atoms
N_aCl	one sodium atom with one chlorine atom
NH_3	two hydrogen atoms with one oxygen atom

2 Choose the correct names from the list below to complete Question **3** on page 118.

- carbon dioxide
- oxygen
- sulfur trioxide
- water
- chlorine
- sulfur
- nitrogen monoxide
- carbon

3 Choose the correct formulae from the list below to complete Questions **4**, **5**, and **6** on pages 118–119.

- O_2
- H_2O
- H
- SO
- Zn_2O_2
- SO_3
- N_aCl
- Cl_2
- N_a
- H_2
- SO_3
- Z_n
- Z_nO

3.1 Three elements

Uses of elements

Learning objectives

- Describe the properties of three elements
- Explain how the uses of three elements are determined by their properties

Questions

1 Describe where on the Periodic Table you will find non-metals.

____

2 Describe the properties of:

a copper

____

b sulfur

____

c germanium

____

3 Give **one** use of:

a copper ______________________________

b sulfur ______________________________

c germanium ______________________________

4 Describe **one** difference between copper and sulfur.

____

5 Describe **one** difference between copper and germanium.

____

6 Describe **one** difference between germanium and sulfur.

____

7 Explain how the properties of copper make it suitable for its use.

____

Support

1 Match each element to its properties. Some properties belong to more than one element.

Element	Properties
1 copper	**A** shiny
	B good conductor of electricity
	C poor conductor of electricity
2 sulfur	**D** easy to shape into thin sheets
	E brittle (breaks easily)
	F dull (not shiny)
3 germanium	**G** can change the direction of light

2 Match each element to its use.

Element	Use
1 copper	**A** used in fibre-optic cables
2 sulfur	**B** used to make fertilizers
3 germanium	**C** used in electricity cables

3.2 Physical properties of metals and non-metals

Practical: Classifying metals and non-metals

Learning objectives

- Use the Periodic Table to find out whether a given element is a metal or non-metal
- Define physical properties
- Describe the physical properties of typical metal and non-metal elements

Safety

- Keep all electrical equipment away from water.
- Do not leave the electrical circuit on when it is not in use.
- Touch the substances very carefully after they have been in hot water, and take care around the beaker of hot water.
- Avoid touching the sharp points on the nails.

Equipment and materials

- metals A, B, C, and D
- non-metals E and F
- 250 cm^3 beaker
- iron nail
- power pack or batteries
- heatproof mat
- three wires
- crocodile clips for connections
- bulb
- timer
- access to hot water tap

Method

Experiment 1: Testing electrical conduction

1. Set up a circuit as shown in the diagram.
2. Place material A between the crocodile clips (one clip on each end) so that the circuit is complete. You should place a heatproof mat under the material while it is being tested.
3. Switch on the power supply.
4. Write your observations in your results table.
5. Repeat the experiment for the rest of the materials B–E, testing each material separately.

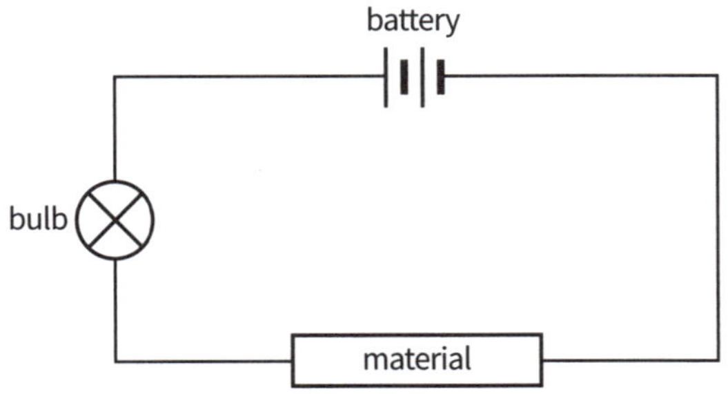

Experiment 2: Testing the material's behaviour

1 Take the material in your hands and try to bend and shape it. Try not to break it.
2 Decide if the material could be described by any of these words: *brittle* (breaks easily), *malleable* (can be shaped easily without breaking), *strong*.
3 Write the words you have chosen in your results table.

Experiment 3: Testing heat conduction

1 Place 100 cm^3 of hot water (not boiling) into a 250 cm^3 beaker.
2 Place your material into the water so that one of the ends is sticking out.
3 After three minutes, carefully feel the end of the material that is out of the water.
4 Write your observations in your results table.
5 Repeat the experiment for all your materials.

Results/Task

Complete the results table below.

Material	Does it conduct electricity? (Does the bulb light?)	Is it brittle, malleable, or strong?	Does it conduct heat well?
metal A			
metal B			
metal C			
metal D			
non-metal E			
non-metal F			

Questions

1 Describe **four** properties of typical metals. ____________________

____

2 Describe **four** properties of typical non-metals. ____________________

____

3 Give the name of elements with properties between those of metals and non-metals.

____

4 Describe the meaning of the term *physical properties*.

____

5 Describe where on the Periodic Table you can find metal elements.

____

6 Describe where on the Periodic Table you can find non-metal elements.

____

7 Tick (✓) the boxes to indicate whether the elements below are metals or non-metals.

	Fluorine	Sodium	Iron	Nickel	Nitrogen
Metal					
Non-metal					

Support

1 Complete the table showing properties of typical metals and non-metals using the words and phrases in the box below.

malleable (can be shaped easily without breaking)	low density	shiny
poor conductor of electricity	good conductor of heat	not sonorous

Properties of a typical metal (when solid)	Properties of a typical non-metal (when solid)
conductor of electricity	
	poor conductor of heat
	dull (not shiny)
high density	
	brittle (breaks easily)
sonorous (rings when hit)	

2 Choose the correct sentence ending to create the definition of *physical properties*.

Sentence starter

1 Physical properties are …

Possible sentence endings

A … how bendy or stretchy a substance is.

B … the properties you can see, feel, or measure without changing the material.

C … how the material reacts with other materials.

D … any properties measured in physics.

3 Match metals and non-metals to their position in the Periodic Table.

Sentence starters

1 Metals …

2 Non-metals …

Possible sentence endings

A … are on the right side of the Periodic Table.

B … are on the left side of the Periodic Table.

3.3 Chemical properties of metals and non-metals

Practical: Reacting metals and non-metals

Learning objectives

- Define chemical properties
- Describe the chemical properties of metals and non-metals

Safety

- Wear safety glasses and keep hair tied back.
- Do not look directly at burning magnesium.
- Blow gently through the straw to avoid splashing, and be careful not to suck through the straw!
- Do not share straws.

Equipment and materials

- small conical flask/boiling tube
- universal indicator
- straw
- limewater and pipette
- spatula
- magnesium oxide powder
- Petri dish
- red litmus paper
- distilled water

Method

Reactions of metals and non-metals with oxygen

Watch your teacher burning magnesium in oxygen and burning sulfur in oxygen. Complete the table with your observations.

Reaction of non-metal oxides with water

1. Use a pipette to add ~ 10 cm^3 of limewater to your conical flask/boiling tube.
2. Add three drops of universal indicator to the limewater. Record the colour of the indicator.
3. Blow GENTLY through your straw into the limewater to add carbon dioxide to the water. Make a note of any colour change you see.

Reaction of metal oxides with water

1. Place a small amount of magnesium oxide powder in the centre of a Petri dish using a spatula.
2. Drop three or four drops of distilled water on top of the magnesium oxide.
3. Put the red litmus paper in the water–magnesium oxide mix and record any observations.

Results

Reaction	Observation of colour change	Is the solution acidic or alkaline?
magnesium + oxygen	The silver metal turns …	X
sulfur + oxygen	The yellow powder turns …	X
carbon dioxide + water	The universal indicator solution turns …	
magnesium oxide + water	Red litmus paper turns …	

Questions

1 Write down the definition of the term *chemical properties*.

____

2 Name the product formed when magnesium reacts with oxygen. ______________________________

3 Give the word equation for the reaction of magnesium and oxygen to make magnesium oxide.

____

4 Describe what colour you would observe when magnesium oxide is dissolved (mixed) in water and red litmus paper is put in the solution.

____

5 Suggest whether this solution is acidic or alkaline. ______________________________

6 Describe the chemical properties of typical metals.

____

____

____

7 Name the product made when sulfur reacts with oxygen. ______________________________

8 Give the word equation for the reaction of sulfur and oxygen to make sulfur dioxide.

____

9 Describe what you would observe when carbon dioxide is dissolved in water and universal indicator added.

____

10 Suggest whether this solution is acidic or alkaline. ______________________________

11 Describe the chemical properties of typical non-metals.

____

____

Support

1 Match the sentence starter with the correct sentence ending to make the definition of the term *chemical properties*.

Sentence starter

1 Chemical properties of a substance …

Sentence endings

A … are the names of the elements that make up the substance.

B … are the properties you can see, feel, or measure without changing the material.

C … describe its chemical reactions.

2 Match the sentence starters with the correct sentence ending to give the chemical properties of metals and non-metals.

Sentence starters

1 Metals …

2 Non-metals …

Sentence endings

A ... react with oxygen to make a non-metal oxide.

B ... react with oxygen to make a metal oxide.

C ... dissolve (mix) in water to make an acidic solution.

D ... dissolve in water to make an alkaline solution.

3.4 Groups and periods

Patterns, groups, and periods in the Periodic Table

Learning objectives

- Give the group and period numbers of elements
- Use data from tables or bar charts to describe patterns in the properties of elements in groups or periods
- Use data to predict the properties of another element in a group or period

Task: Patterns in elements

In the table below, there are descriptions of 12 elements.

1 Group these elements together in as many different ways as you can, using only these descriptions.

2 Write down the groups and describe what the elements in each group have in common.

Hydrogen a colourless gas explosive (reactive) when burned	**Chlorine** a green gas reacts easily with other elements	**Neon** a colourless gas does not react very much at all
Argon a colourless gas does not react very much at all	**Sodium** a soft grey solid floats on water and reacts easily	**Potassium** a soft grey solid floats on water and reacts vigorously
Calcium a silver–grey solid reacts steadily with water	**Helium** a colourless gas does not react very much at all	**Fluorine** a green gas reacts vigorously with other elements
Magnesium a silver–grey solid reacts slowly with water	**Bromine** red–brown liquid reacts steadily with other elements	**Lithium** a soft grey solid floats on water and reacts easily

Questions

1 Name the columns in the Periodic Table. ________________

2 Name the rows in the Periodic Table. ________________

3 Using the Periodic Table, give the group and period of these elements:

a carbon ________

b sodium ________

c helium ________

d nitrogen ________

e magnesium ________

f chlorine ________

4 Name the elements found in these positions in the Periodic Table.

a Group 1, Period 1 ________

b Group 1, Period 2 ________

c Group 2, Period 4 ________

d Group 3, Period 3 ________

e Group 0, Period 2 ________

5 The three tables below show density data for elements near zirconium in the Periodic Table. Each table shows the elements in one group.

a Choose the correct **bold** word to complete the sentence below. The sentence describes the pattern in the data for the second table.

The density of the elements **increases** / **decreases** as you go down the group.

b Use the data to predict the approximate density of zirconium.

Element	Density in g/cm^3
titanium	4.5
zirconium	
hafnium	13.3

Element	Density in g/cm^3
vanadium	6.0
nobelium	8.6
tantalum	16.4

Element	Density in g/cm^3
chromium	7.15
molybdenum	10.2
tungsten	19.3

6 The table below shows the density of three elements in the same group of the Periodic Table. Describe the pattern in density from the top to the bottom of the group.

Element	Density in g/cm^3
copper	8.96
silver	10.49
gold	19.32

____

____

3.5 The elements of Group 1

CHEMISTRY

Practical: How do Group 1 elements react?

Learning objectives

- Describe the physical properties of the Group 1 elements
- Use data from tables or bar charts to describe patterns in the melting and boiling points of the Group 1 elements
- Use patterns to predict reactions of the Group 1 elements with water

Safety

- Wear chemical splash-proof safety glasses.
- Remain 2–3 metres away from the safety screen until told otherwise.

Task

Your teacher will show you how the first three Group 1 elements react with water. Record your observations in the table below.

Results

Group 1 element	Reactions
lithium	
sodium	
potassium	

Questions

1 Suggest whether Group 1 elements are metals or non-metals.

____

2 Explain your answer to Question **1** using their position in the Periodic Table.

____

3 Name the gas produced in the reactions of lithium, sodium, and potassium with water.

____

4 Describe **three** physical properties of Group 1 elements that they share with other metals.

____

____

5 Describe **two** physical properties of Group 1 elements that are different from other metals.

6 Choose the correct **bold** word to complete the sentence below.
The reactions of Group 1 elements with water get **more** / **less** vigorous (strong) as you go down the group.

7 Predict whether the reaction of rubidium with water will be more or less vigorous than the reaction of potassium with water.

8 Here is the word equation for the reaction of lithium with water:
lithium + water → lithium hydroxide + hydrogen

a Write the word equation for the reaction of sodium with water.

b Write the word equation for the reaction of potassium with water.

9 The table below shows the melting points of Group 1 elements.

Group 1 element	Melting point in °C
lithium	180
sodium	98
potassium	64
rubidium	39

a Plot these melting points on a bar chart.

b Use your bar chart to describe the pattern in the melting points of Group 1 elements as you go down the group.

10 The table below shows the boiling points of Group 1 elements as you go down the group. Describe how the boiling points change as you go from the top to the bottom of the group.

Group 1 element	Boiling point in °C
lithium	1330
sodium	890
potassium	774
rubidium	688

____

____

Support

1 Choose the correct physical properties of Group 1 elements from the list below.

- insulators of heat and electricity
- soft
- shiny
- lower melting points than other metals
- dull (not shiny)
- hard
- good conductors of heat and electricity
- higher melting points than other metals

2 Choose the correct **bold** words to complete the sentences below. These sentences describe the patterns in the melting and boiling points of Group 1 elements.

The melting points of Group 1 elements **increase / decrease** as you go down the group.

The boiling points of Group 1 elements **increase / decrease** as you go down the group.

3.6 The elements of Group 7

Exploring Group 7 elements

Learning objectives

- Describe the physical properties of the Group 7 elements
- Use data from tables or bar charts to describe patterns in the melting and boiling points of the Group 7 elements
- Use patterns to predict reactions of the Group 7 elements with iron

Task

Read the information below about the Group 7 elements. Use the information to complete the table.

Group 7

The Group 7 elements are called the halogens. They are fluorine, chlorine, bromine, iodine, and astatine. Group 7 is found on the right side of the Periodic Table, so the Group 7 elements are all non-metal elements. A typical property of non-metals is their low melting and boiling points, and Group 7 elements follow this trend. Chlorine's melting point is −101 °C and its boiling point is −35 °C, so it is a gas at room temperature. The melting point of bromine is −7 °C and its boiling point is 59 °C, so it is a dark red liquid at room temperature. Iodine has a higher melting point than bromine and chlorine; it melts at 114 °C and boils at 184 °C. Therefore, it is still in the solid state at room temperature.

The halogens form salts when they react with metals, and they all react similarly to each other. When iron reacts with chlorine, it produces iron chloride; when iron reacts with bromine, it produces iron bromide; and iron iodide is produced in the reaction of iron and iodine. The halogens have lots of uses: they can kill bacteria and microbes, so they are often used to sterilize water and cuts, and to make pesticides and plastics.

Group 1 element	Colour	State at room temperature	Melting point in °C	Boiling point in °C	Reactive or unreactive?	Product when reacted with iron
chlorine						
bromine						
iodine						

Questions

1 Describe the colours and states at room temperature of chlorine, bromine, and iodine.

2 Identify if Group 7 elements have high or low melting points.

---

3 Use data from the table to describe the pattern in the melting points of the Group 7 elements as you go down the group.

---

4 Use data from the table to describe the pattern in the boiling points of the Group 7 elements as you go down the group.

---

5 Iron reacts with chlorine to form iron chloride. Here is the word equation:

iron + chlorine → iron chloride

a Describe the reactions of the Group 7 elements with iron.

---

b Write the word equation for the reaction of iron and iodine to make iron iodide.

---

c Predict the product formed when iron reacts with bromine.

---

6 The reaction of iron with chlorine is very vigorous (strong), the reaction of iron with bromine is not very vigorous, and the reaction of iron with iodine is not vigorous at all. Describe the pattern of reactivity in Group 7.

Support

1 Match each Group 7 element to its colour and its state at room temperature.

Group 7 element	**Colour**	**State at room temperature**
chlorine	pale green	solid
bromine	grey	liquid
iodine	dark red	gas

2 Tick (✓) the correct description of the pattern in the melting points of the Group 7 elements as you go down the group.

- ☐ The melting points of the Group 7 elements are all very similar.
- ☐ The melting points of the Group 7 elements increase as you go down the group.
- ☐ The melting points of the Group 7 elements decrease as you go down the group.
- ☐ The melting points of the Group 7 elements are all completely different; there is no pattern.

3 Tick (✓) the correct description of the pattern in the boiling points of the Group 7 elements as you go down the group.

- ☐ The boiling points of the Group 7 elements are all very similar.
- ☐ The boiling points of the Group 7 elements increase as you go down the group.
- ☐ The boiling points of the Group 7 elements decrease as you go down the group.
- ☐ The boiling points of the Group 7 elements are all completely different; there is no pattern.

3.7 The elements of Group 0

Trends in the noble gases

Learning objectives

- Describe the physical properties of the Group 0 elements
- Use data from tables or bar charts to describe patterns in the melting and boiling points of the Group 0 elements
- Use patterns to predict properties of the Group 0 elements, and their uses

Task

Use the data in the table below to plot the boiling points of the Group 0 elements in a bar chart.

Element	Boiling point in °C
helium	−269
neon	−246
argon	−186
krypton	−152
xenon	−108

Questions

1 Describe the position of the noble gases in the Periodic Table.

2 Choose the correct **bold** words to describe the chemical properties of the Group 0 elements.
The Group 0 elements are all **reactive / unreactive**, and they get **more / less** reactive as you go down the group.

3 Describe the meaning of the key word *unreactive*.

4 Describe the physical properties of the Group 0 elements, including their colour, state, and their melting and boiling points.

5 Match each Group 0 element to its common use.

Group 0	**Common use**
1 helium	**A** in light-up advertising signs
2 argon	**B** in balloons
3 neon	**C** in the space between sheets of glass in a double-glazed window

6 Explain how the properties of the Group 0 elements helium, argon, and neon make them suitable for their uses.

7 Use your bar graph to describe the pattern in boiling points of the Group 0 elements.

8 Use the bar chart below to describe the pattern in melting points of the Group 0 elements.

____

____

____

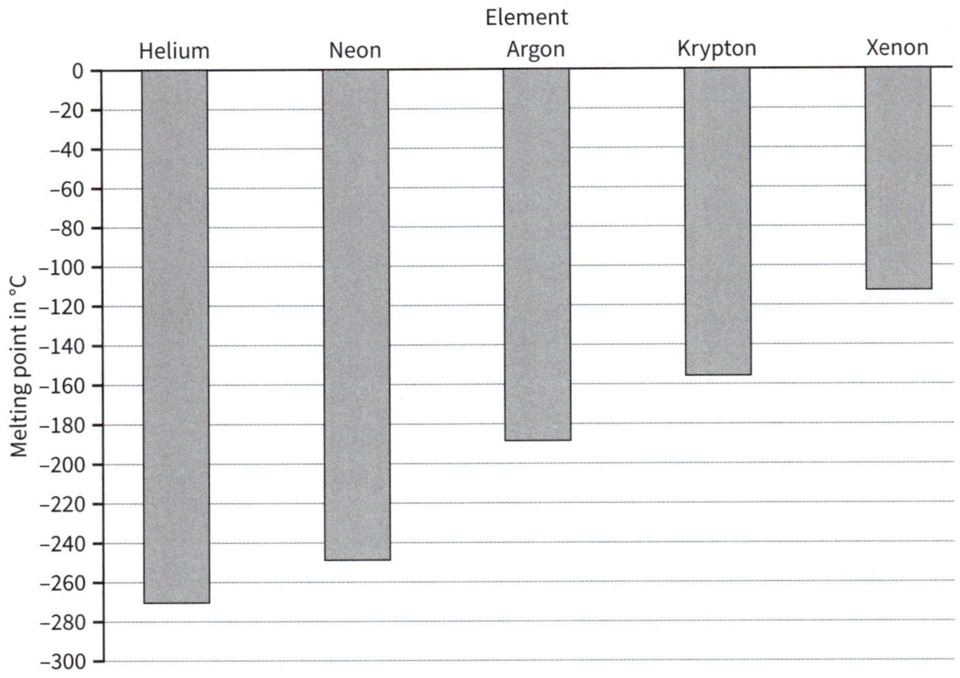

Support

1 Choose the correct description of the physical properties of Group 0 elements from the lists below.

a Colour and state

- The Group 0 elements are all brightly coloured substances in the solid state at room temperature.
- The Group 0 elements are all colourless substances in the solid state at room temperature.
- The Group 0 elements are all colourless substances in the gas state at room temperature.

b Melting / boiling point

- The Group 0 elements have low melting and boiling points.
- The Group 0 elements have high melting and boiling points.
- The Group 0 elements have low melting points and high boiling points.

2 Match the sentence starters to the correct sentence endings. The sentences describe the patterns in the melting and boiling points of the Group 0 elements.

Sentence starters	Sentence endings
1 As you go down the group, the melting points of the Group 0 elements …	**A** … increase.
2 As you go down the group, the boiling points of the Group 0 elements …	**B** … decrease.
	C … stay the same.

4.1 Acids and alkalis

Using acids and alkalis safely

Learning objectives

- Describe the hazards of using acids and alkalis
- State how to control the risks of using acids
- Compare concentrated and dilute solutions

Task

Scientists use hazard symbols to label the risks linked with a chemical. New hazard symbols are being introduced so that every scientist uses the same hazard symbols.

Complete the table on the following page. Fill it in using the correct names of properties and descriptions from the following options.

Property

corrosive	health hazard (harmful)	explosive	flammable	toxic	caution (irritant)

Descriptions

This may dissolve or burn materials, including skin.

This includes irritants, harmful (dangerous) substances, and some low-hazard substances.

This contains dangerous organisms such as bacteria.

This can be poisonous and possibly cause death.

This may explode.

This can catch fire easily.

Old hazard symbol	New hazard symbol	Property	Description

Questions

1 Match each sentence halves.

1	A hazard is …	**A**	… an image used to give information about the dangers of a chemical.
2	A hazard symbol is …	**B**	… anything that can cause you harm (hurt you).

2 A scientist wants to use some hydrochloric acid and sodium hydroxide for an experiment. They both have the following hazard symbol on the label:

a Name the hazard symbol.

____

b Describe **two** hazards linked to using concentrated hydrochloric acid.

____

____

____

c Describe how the scientist can control the risks from these hazards.

____

____

Support

1 Draw lines to match the hazard symbols to their name and description.

Old hazard symbol	New hazard symbol	Property	Description
		corrosive	This may dissolve or burn materials, including skin.
		health hazard (harmful)	This includes irritants, harmful (dangerous) substances, and some low-hazard substances.
		explosive	This contains dangerous organisms such as bacteria.
		flammable	This can be poisonous and possibly cause death.
		toxic	This may explode.
		caution (irritant)	This can catch fire easily.

2 Choose the correct **two** hazards (dangers) linked to using concentrated hydrochloric acid from the list below.

- can burn your skin
- can catch fire easily
- may explode
- can burn or damage your eyes
- can poison you

3 Choose the best ways to control the risks from these hazards from the list below.

- Keep away from naked flames.
- Wear steel toe-capped shoes.
- Wear goggles/safety glasses.
- Keep windows and doors open.
- Wear a face mask.
- Wash any spillages off skin with plenty of water.
- Keep the temperature of the laboratory below 20 °c.
- Keep the lid on the acid when it is not in use.
- Do not touch the solutions.

4.2 Indicators and pH

Practical: Using universal indicator

Learning objectives

- Determine whether a solution is acidic or alkaline, given its colour in indicator
- Identify acids, alkalis, and neutral solutions on the pH scale
- Use universal indicator to measure the pH of a solution

Safety

- Wear safety glasses and keep hair tied back.
- Solutions A, B, C, and D are irritants, so avoid contact with the skin.
- Universal indicator is harmful (dangerous) and can easily catch fire.

Equipment and materials

- spotting tile
- six universal indicator paper strips
- small bottle of universal indicator solution
- universal indicator colour comparison chart
- solutions A, B, C, D, E, and F with pipettes

Method

1. Use a pipette to place a few drops of solution A in one of the wells in a spotting tile.
2. Carefully place the end of a universal indicator strip into the solution (do not let it get too wet).
3. Record the colour you observe and use the comparison chart to decide the pH.
4. Add a drop of universal indicator solution to the solution in the well.
5. Note the colour and use the comparison chart to decide the pH.
6. Repeat the above steps for all solutions, B to F, using a clean and empty well each time. Record your results.

Results

Solution	Observation with universal indicator paper	Likely pH value?	Observation with universal indicator solution	Likely pH value?
A				
B				
C				
D				
E				
F				

Questions

1 State the colour change of litmus paper in acidic solutions. ______

2 State the colour change of litmus paper in alkaline solutions. ______

3 Match the range on the pH scale to whether it shows a solution is acidic, neutral, or alkaline.

Range		Solution	
1	a pH of more than 7	A	neutral
2	a pH of less than 7	B	alkaline
3	a pH of 7	C	acidic

4 State the correct order for these statements to describe how to use universal indicator to determine the pH of a solution.

A	Add a drop of universal indicator to the solution on the watch glass.	
B	Match the colour observed to the pH scale to determine the pH.	
C	Record the colour you observe.	
D	Place a few drops of your unknown solution onto a watch glass.	

5 From your results, state which of the solutions, A to F, are acidic (if any). ______

6 From your results, state which of the solutions, A to F, are neutral (if any). ______

7 From your results, state which of the solutions, A to F, are alkaline (if any). ______

8 Describe how you might measure a more accurate pH of a solution.

______

Applications of pH testing

Some plants can produce different coloured flowers in more acidic soil. Hydrangeas produce blue flowers in soil of about pH 5, and pink flowers in soil of about pH 6.

A flower farmer tests the pH of the soil from three different fields, using universal indicator. His observations are shown in the table below.

Soil sample	Observation with universal indicator
Field 1	dark green
Field 2	yellow/orange
Field 3	green/blue

1 State the likely pH value of:

a Field 1 ______ b Field 2 ______ c Field 3 ______

2 Suggest which field the flower farmer should use to plant his hydrangeas to have the best chance of producing blue flowers.

______

4.3 Neutralization

Practical: Neutralizing stomach acid

Learning objectives

- Define a base and an alkali
- Describe how pH changes in neutralization reactions
- Give examples of useful neutralization reactions

Safety

- Wear safety glasses throughout the practical activity.
- The hydrochloric acid is an irritant, so avoid contact with skin.
- Indigestion remedy A is an irritant.
- Indigestion remedy B is an irritant.
- Universal indicator solution is harmful (dangerous) and can easily catch fire.

Equipment and materials

- hydrochloric acid
- indigestion remedy A
- indigestion remedy B
- universal indicator solution
- pipettes
- two glass beakers
- two 25 cm^3 measuring cylinders

Method

1. Place 5 cm^3 of indigestion remedy A into a glass beaker.
2. Add two drops of universal indicator solution.
3. Use a pipette to add hydrochloric acid, drop by drop, to the indigestion remedy until the solution is neutralized.
4. Record how many drops of acid you used to neutralize the indigestion remedy.
5. Repeat the method for indigestion remedy B. Record your results.

Results

Indigestion remedy	Number of drops of hydrochloric acid needed to neutralize it
A	
B	

Questions

1 Name **four** variables in this experiment.

2 Identify the independent variable that is being changed.

3 Identify the dependent variable that is being measured.

4 Identify **two** control variables that are being kept the same.

5 State how you know when the remedy has neutralized the acid.

6 Write down the definition of a base.

7 Write down the definition of an alkali.

8 Describe a neutralization reaction.

9 Describe the pH range for acidic substances.

10 Describe the pH range for alkaline substances.

11 Describe the pH range for neutral substances.

12 Describe how the pH changed when you added the hydrochloric acid to the alkaline indigestion remedy.

13 Give **two** examples of useful neutralization reactions.

____

____

14 Identify which indigestion remedy is better at neutralizing stomach acid.

____

15 Explain how you know this.

____

____

Support

1 Draw lines to match the variables.

independent variable being measured	type of acid being added
dependent variable being changed	type of indigestion remedy
control variable being kept the same	number of drops of acid being added

2 Draw lines to match the key words *base*, *alkali*, and *neutralization* to their definition.

base	a substance that neutralizes an acid
alkali	a reaction where an acid reacts with a substance to cancel it out
neutralization	a base that dissolves

3 Choose examples of useful neutralization reactions from this list of useful chemical reactions.

- adding base to over-acidic soil to increase the pH
- burning methane in oxygen to produce carbon dioxide and water
- using alkaline toothpaste to brush teeth after eating and drinking
- digesting food
- respiration
- putting vinegar on an alkaline wasp sting to decrease the pH
- photosynthesis
- adding base to acidic lakes to increase the pH

4.4 Making salts

Practical: Making magnesium chloride

Learning objectives

- Explain what a salt is in science
- Predict the salt that forms when an acid reacts with a metal or base
- Describe how to make a given salt from an acid and a metal or insoluble base

Safety

- Wear safety glasses and keep hair tied up throughout the practical.
- Make sure you heat the evaporating dish gently – your teacher will show you how to do this.
- Make sure you do not touch any hot equipment until it has cooled down.
- Hydrochloric acid is an irritant. Wash any spills off your skin immediately.
- The salt formed is NOT safe to eat.

Equipment and materials

- hydrochloric acid
- strips of magnesium metal
- pipettes
- 50 cm^3 beaker
- piece of filter paper
- funnel
- 50 cm^3 conical flask
- evaporating basin
- tripod
- gauze
- Bunsen burner
- heatproof mat
- universal indicator strips

Method

1 Pour 20 cm^3 of hydrochloric acid into your beaker.
2 Add one magnesium strip.
3 Observe the fizzing/effervescence. If the fizzing stops and there is still magnesium left in the beaker, continue to Step **4**. If not, add another strip and repeat this step. (Make sure that all the reactions between magnesium and hydrochloric acid have been completed before lighting any Bunsen burners.)
4 Pour the solution through filter paper in a filter funnel, to remove the extra magnesium.
5 Use a pipette to place a single drop of the salt solution onto a strip of universal indicator paper.
6 Record the pH of the salt solution.
7 Set up your equipment as shown in the diagram.
8 Place the salt solution into the evaporating basin. Heat gently until some of the water evaporates – be careful of the solution spitting.

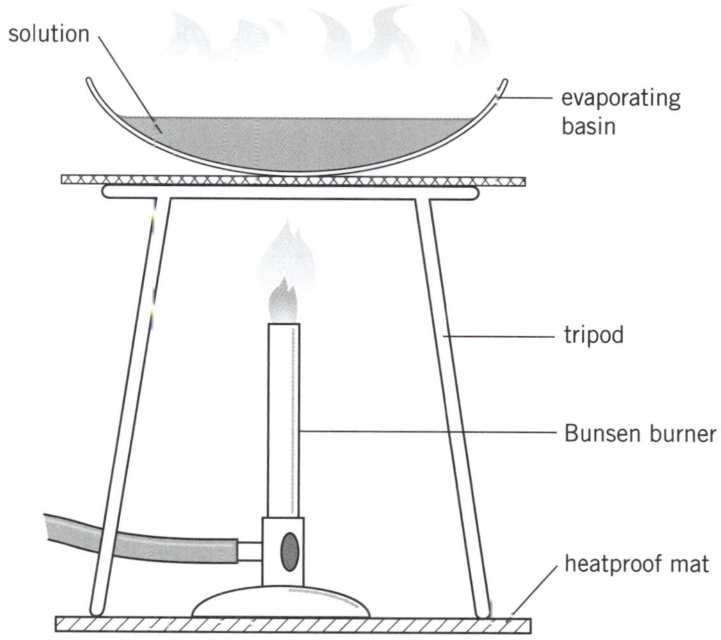

9 Reduce the heat when half of the solution has evaporated.
10 Turn off the Bunsen burner when about two-thirds of the solution has evaporated.
11 Do not touch the hot equipment until it has cooled down and you are told to do so.

Results

Record the pH of the solution in your beaker. pH = ____________________

Questions

1 State the names of the **two** reactants you used.

____

2 State the names of the **two** products that were formed.

____

3 Write the word equation for this reaction.

____

4 Identify whether the solution in your beaker is an acidic, neutral, or alkaline solution.

____

5 Name this type of reaction.

____

6 Write down the definition of *salt* in chemistry.

____

7 Predict the name of the salt made when hydrochloric acid reacts with calcium.

____

8 Predict the name of the salt made when sodium hydroxide reacts with nitric acid.

____

9 Describe the steps needed to make magnesium chloride from hydrochloric acid and magnesium oxide powder.

____

____

____

____

____

____

Support

1 Choose the correct sentence ending to make the definition of *salt* in science.

A salt is … … a substance made up of two different elements joined together.

… a compound that forms when an acid reacts with a metal element or compound.

… a substance that you put on your chips.

… a substance made up of two or more atoms joined together.

2 Choose the correct salts from the box to answer Questions **7** and **8** on page 148.

magnesium chloride	copper oxide	copper sulfate	calcium chloride	calcium sulfate
calcium nitrate	sodium nitrate	magnesium nitrate	sodium chloride	

3 Put these statements in the correct order to describe how to make magnesium chloride from hydrochloric acid and magnesium oxide powder.

A	Add magnesium oxide powder to the beaker and mix.
B	Filter to remove the extra, unreacted magnesium oxide.
C	Add hydrochloric acid to a beaker
D	Leave the evaporating basin in a warm place to allow the rest of the water to evaporate and the crystals to form
E	Keep adding the magnesium oxide until some is left over.
F	Heat the solution in an evaporating basin until half of the water evaporates.

1.1 Introduction to forces

PHYSICS

Practical: Using a newton meter

Learning objectives

- Use force arrows to explain what forces do
- Compare different types of force
- Describe how to measure forces and give the unit of force

Safety

- Take care when lifting heavy objects.
- Use newton meters sensibly so as not to break them.
- Be careful not to drop masses or any heavy objects you may be working with.

Equipment and materials

- newton meters with suitable scales
- pencil case with zip
- mass hangers and masses (10 g and 100 g)
- drawer/cupboard door handle
- two magnets, one with string tied around it to make a loop
- small spring
- block of wood with string tied around it to make a loop
- other suitable objects with string tied around them to make a loop

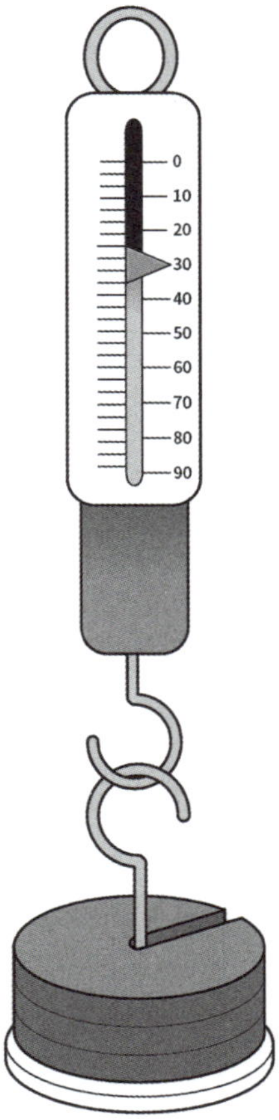

Method

1. Working in pairs, attach the object to the hook of your newton meter.
2. Use the newton meter to measure the force needed to carry out these actions:
   - **a** lift the objects up
   - **b** pull the zip of your pencil case open or closed
   - **c** pull the drawer or cupboard door open
   - **d** pull the two magnets apart
   - **e** pull an object along the bench
   - **f** pull the spring to double its length

   Record your results in the results table.
3. Look around you. Find some other small objects that you can attach to your newton meter. Measure the force needed to lift these objects and record these in your results table.

Results

Action	Force needed to carry out the action (N)

Questions

1 List the actions in order of size of the force required.

2 Describe how you would use a newton meter to take accurate measurements.

1.2 Squashing and stretching

Practical: Stretching springs

Learning objectives

- Describe how forces deform (change the shape of) objects
- Explain how solid surfaces provide a support force

Safety

- Wear safety glasses.
- Make sure the spring is fastened well to the clamp stand.
- Make sure you arrange the boss head of the clamp stand over the metal base.
- Do not make the masses bounce up and down on the spring.
- Make sure masses do not fall onto the floor or onto people's feet.

Equipment and materials

- metre ruler
- clamp stand
- ruler
- small spring with suitable elastic limit
- 1 N weights and a hanger
- safety glasses
- G-clamp (used to keep clamp stands from falling over)

Method

1 Predict what will happen to the extension of the spring when more weights are added.
2 Use the G-clamp to fix the clamp stand securely to the bench.
3 Hang the spring carefully off the clamp so that the spring hangs over the side of the bench without touching it.
4 Measure the original length of the spring with no force acting on it.
5 Hang the 1 N hanger from the spring.
6 Measure the new length of the spring and record it in your results table.
7 Add 1 N weights to the spring, one at a time, and measure the new length of the spring each time. Record it in your results table.
8 Repeat step **7**, until a total weight of 5 N is reached.

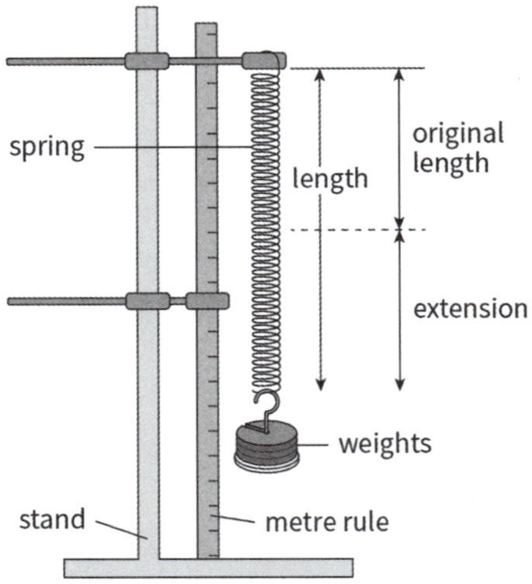

Results

1 Record your measurements in the table.

Force (N)	New length (cm)	Original length (cm)	Extension (cm) (new length – original length)

2 Calculate the extension for each force added to the spring and write it in the table.

3 Plot your results on a graph. The *x*-axis scale is for the force (in N) and the *y*-axis scale is for the extension (in cm). Draw a straight line of best fit through your points.

Questions

1 Describe the pattern in your results. Use numbers in your answer, if possible.

____

____

2 Do your results match your prediction? Explain your answer.

____

____

3 Describe **one** way in which you could improve your experiment.

____

____

1.3 Drag forces and friction

Practical: Investigating friction

Learning objectives

- Describe the effects of drag forces and friction
- Explain how drag forces and friction occur
- Describe how drag forces and friction can be reduced

Safety

- Be careful not to slip if you have taken off your shoe.
- Use newton meters sensibly so as not to break them.
- Be careful when lifting objects to avoid dropping heavy objects onto fingers/feet.

Equipment and materials

- newton meters with suitable scales
- suitable objects to drag (e.g. wooden block with circle of string)
- string
- different surfaces (e.g. carpet, heatproof mat, sandpaper, floor)

Method

1. Predict which surface will have the most friction and which will have the least friction.
2. Attach the object/shoe to the hook of your newton meter.

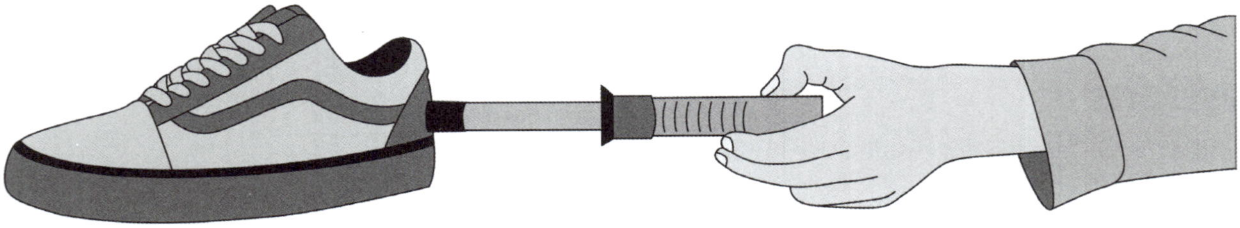

3. Choose a surface to place your object on.
4. Use the newton meter to measure the size of the force needed so that the object just starts to move along the surface. (It must not lift off the surface.)
5. Record your results in the table.

Results

Prediction: The surface with the most friction will be ______________________.

The surface with the least friction will be ______________________.

Type of surface	Force needed to start the object moving (N)

Questions

1 Which surface had the most friction? Explain your answer.

____

____

2 Which surface had the least friction? Explain your answer.

____

____

3 Do your results match your prediction? Explain your answer.

____

____

4 Suggest **two** controlled variables in your experiment.

____

____

5 Describe **one** way that you could improve your experiment.

____

____

6 Suggest **one** possible source of error in your experiment.

____

7 Explain why friction occurs.

____

____

1.4 Forces at a distance

Practical: Investigating mass and weight

Learning objectives

- Describe the effects of fields
- Describe the difference between weight and mass
- Calculate weight

Safety

- Be careful not to drop the masses.
- Use newton meters sensibly so as not to break them.

Equipment and materials

- newton meters with suitable scales
- 100 g masses
- mass holders
- balance
- objects of known mass

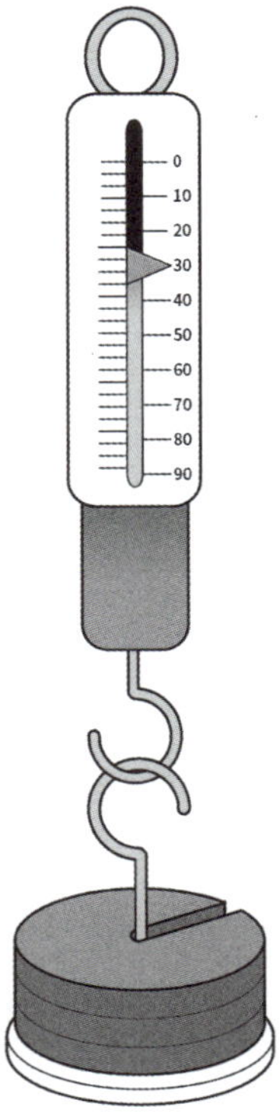

Method

1 Attach the mass hanger with 0.1 kg (100 g) mass to the hook of your newton meter.

2 Use the newton meter to measure the weight of the mass.

3 Repeat for 0.2 kg, 0.3 kg, 0.4 kg, and 0.5 kg.

4 Record your results in the table.

Results

Mass (kg)	Weight (N)

Questions

1 What is the weight of a 0.1 kg mass?

____

2 What is the difference between mass and weight?

____

____

3 What pattern do you notice in your results? (**Hint:** What do you have to multiply the mass by to calculate the weight?)

____

____

4 Complete the equation linking weight and mass.

__________ (in N) = __________ (in kg) × gravitational field strength (in N/kg)

5 Describe **one** way in which you could improve your experiment.

____

6 Calculate the weight of an object with a mass of 1.5 kg.

Weight = __________ N

7 Calculate the weight of an object with a mass of 1200 g. (**Hint:** Check the units are correct.)

Weight = __________ N

Support

1 a Write down the equation linking mass and weight.

__________ (in N) = __________ (in kg) × gravitational field strength (in N/kg)

b Write down the equation with the numbers from the question.

Weight = __________ × __________

c Work out the weight in newtons.

Weight = __________ N

1.5 Balanced and unbalanced

PHYSICS

Practical: Exploring the forces around us

Learning objectives

- Describe the difference between balanced and unbalanced forces
- Explain why an object is in equilibrium
- Explain the changing motion of objects

Safety

- Be careful not to spill water. Clear up any spills immediately with a paper towel.

Equipment and materials

- small ball
- floating object
- car and ramp
- book
- bung hanging from string

Method

Carry out actions **a–f** as experiments. Record your results, as described in steps **1–3**, in the table.

a dropping a ball
b floating a boat
c car going up a ramp
d car doing down a ramp
e book on desk
f rubber bung hanging from string

1. Record the names of the forces acting in each experiment. Choose from: gravity, upthrust, weight, air resistance, tension, friction, reaction force.
2. Record the motion of the object. Choose from: speeding up, slowing down, constant speed (speed that does not change), staying still.
3. Draw a force diagram for each experiment. When drawing the force diagrams, use a dot to represent the object. Make sure the size of each arrow indicates which is the larger force, or if the forces are the same size. Do not draw force diagrams for the car going up or down the ramp.

Results

Experiment	Names of forces	Balanced or unbalanced	Motion of object	Force diagram
				 (dot to represent object)

Questions

1 Describe the motion of an object if the forces acting on it are balanced.

____

____

2 Describe the motion of an object if the forces acting on it are unbalanced.

____

____

3 Explain what it means when an object is in equilibrium.

____

____

2.1 Waves

PHYSICS

Slinkys and fish tanks

Learning objectives

- Describe the properties of waves
- Describe how waves are reflected and superpose

Task

Your teacher will show you ways of making different types of wave.
Observe the waves carefully and complete the questions.

Observations and questions

1 Describe how the cork on the surface of the water moves as the wave passes.

____

2 Describe how the water moves as the wave passes.

____

3 Describe how the coils on the Slinky spring move as the wave passes.

____

4 Describe what happens to the water waves when they hit the barrier.

____

5 Complete the definition of a wave.

A wave is an oscillation or _______________ that transfers (moves) _______________ without the matter itself being transferred.

6 Explain how you can tell that a water wave transfers energy, but the water itself does not get transferred.

____

____

Support

For Question **6**, choose your answer from these three options:

A The cork moves up and down, but it does not move across the ripple tank.
B The cork moves up and down, and it also moves across the ripple tank.
C The cork moves across the ripple tank, but it does not move up and down.

2.2 Sound

Practical: Investigating sound

Learning objectives

- Describe how sound is produced and travels
- Use the particle model to explain why the speed of sound is different in different materials

Task

1 Work your way around the 'sound circus' set up by your teacher. Follow the instructions and answer the questions provided with each object.

2 Watch your classmates behaving as particles to show how sound travels through solids, liquids, and gases.

Observations and questions

1 Describe what all of the objects that produce a sound have in common.

____

2 Describe how students can model a sound wave passing through different substances.

____

____

3 Fill in the boxes to show how particles are arranged in solids, in liquids, and in gases.
Use a circle to represent a particle.

Solid	Liquid	Gas

4 The table below shows the speeds of sound in different materials.

Substance	Speed of sound (m/s)	Type of substance
aluminium	6400	solid
air	340	gas
substance A	1500	?
wood	3600	solid
glycerol	1900	liquid
substance B	5800	?
brick	4200	solid
mercury	1450	liquid
helium	970	gas
substance C	260	?

a State the speed of sound in air. Give the units.

____

b Which substance does the sound travel fastest through?

____

c Use the information in the table to determine whether sound travels fastest in solids, liquids, or gases.

____

____

d Suggest which of substances A, B, and C is a solid, a liquid, and a gas.

substance A = ______________________________

substance B = ______________________________

substance C = ______________________________

Support

Use this table to record your observations.

Object	What is vibrating?

2.3 Loudness and pitch

PHYSICS

Changing amplitude and frequency

Learning objectives

- Describe the link between loudness and amplitude of sound waves
- Describe the link between frequency and pitch of sound waves

Task

1 Your teacher will show you how changing the amplitude and frequency of a sound will affect the loudness and pitch.

2 Watch the waves on the oscilloscope carefully and answer the questions.

Questions

1 a State which feature of a sound wave determines the loudness of the sound.

____

b Describe what the wave for a loud sound looks like.

____

2 a State which feature of a sound wave determines the pitch of the sound.

____

b Describe what the wave for a high-pitched sound looks like.

____

3 Complete the sentences with the correct units.

a Frequency is measured in

______________________________.

b Sound intensity (loudness) is measured in

______________________________.

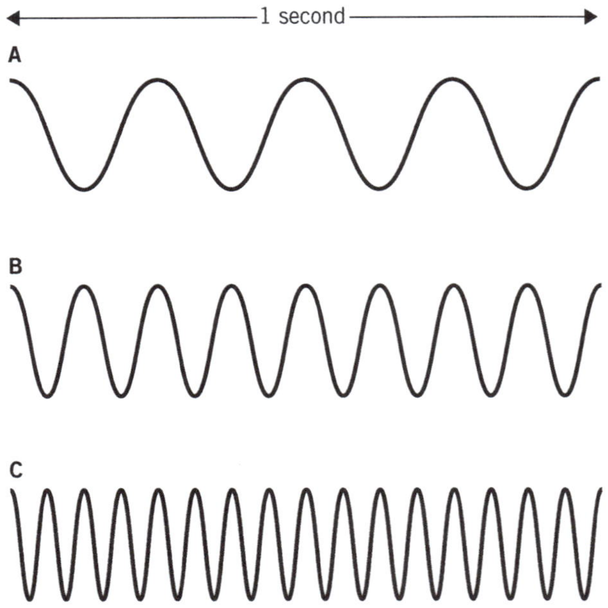

4 The diagram shows the waveforms for three different sounds.

a State which wave has the highest pitch. Give a reason for your answer.

Wave ______________________________

Reason: ______________________________

____

b State which wave has the lowest pitch. Give a reason for your answer.

Wave ______________________________

Reason: ______________________________

5 The diagram shows the waveforms for two different sounds.

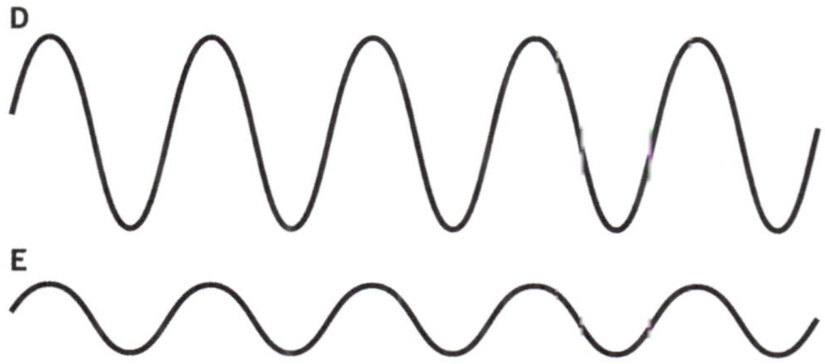

State which wave has the louder sound. Give a reason for your answer.

Wave ______________________________

Reason: ______________________________

Support

For Questions **1a** and **2a**, choose your answer from these words:

amplitude	crest	frequency	trough

For Question **4**, choose the correct letter/word in **bold** to complete the sentences.

Wave **A | B | C** has the highest pitch because its **amplitude | crest | frequency** is the **highest | lowest**.
Wave **A | B | C** has the lowest pitch because its **amplitude | crest | frequency** is the **highest | lowest**.

For Question **5**, choose the correct letter/word in **bold** to complete the sentences.

Wave **D | E** has the loudest sound because its **amplitude | crest | frequency** is the **biggest | smallest**.

2.4 Detecting sound

Ears, microphones, and audible range

Learning objectives

- Describe how the ear works
- Compare the range of human hearing with that of different animals
- Describe how a simple microphone works

Task

Your teacher will show you a model of an ear.
Then they will show you a microphone.
Finally, you will discuss how hearing ranges are different between different animals.

Questions

1 a Using the diagram match the correct letter to the part of the ear.

Ear part	Letter
auditory canal	E
auditory nerve	A
cochlea	C
eardrum	B
pinna	D

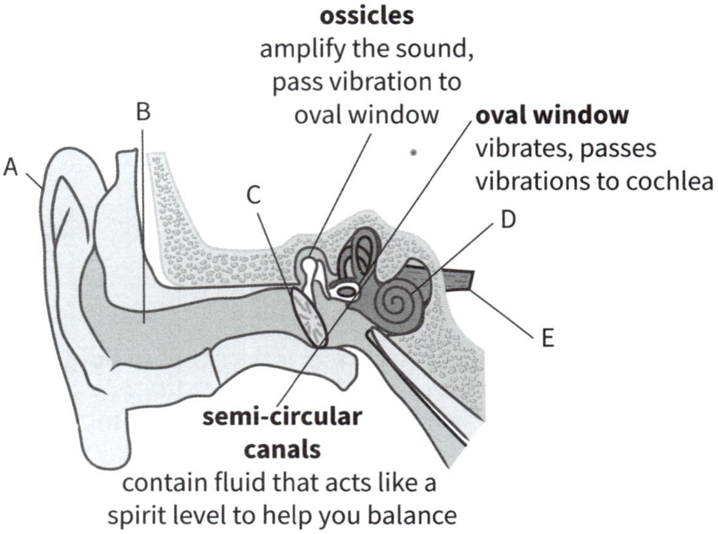

b Describe what each part of the ear does.

- **auditory canal** ______________________________
____
- **auditory nerve** ______________________________
____
- **cochlea** ______________________________
____
- **eardrum** ______________________________
____
- **pinna** ______________________________
____

c Add the parts of the ear to the correct column in the table below.

auditory canal	cochlea	eardrum	pinna

Outer ear	Middle ear	Inner ear
	ossicles oval window	semi-circular canal

2 The table below gives information about animals and the sounds they make and hear.
The loudness of sounds is measured in decibels (dB). The loudest sound has the most decibels.

Animal	Hearing range (Hz)	Loudest sound produced (dB)
human	20–20 000	90
dog	40–60 000	113
elephant	10–10 000	117
howler monkey	100–30 000	140
cat	30–50 000	100
bat	3000–120 000	100

a Name the animal that can hear the highest sounds. ______

b Name the animal that can hear the lowest sounds. ______

c Name the animal that can make the loudest sounds. ______

d Name **two** animals that can hear sounds that are too high for humans to hear.

1: ______

2: ______

e Explain why bats can hear more sounds than any other animal in the table.

______

______

3 a Using the diagram below write the correct letter for the part of the microphone.

Diaphragm ______

Magnet ______

Sound waves ______

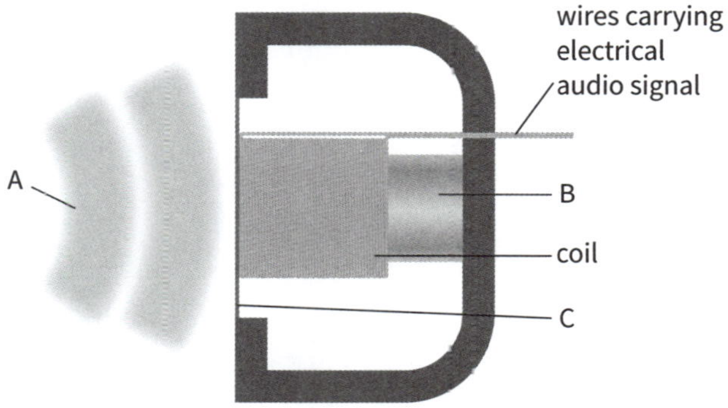

b Complete the sentences to describe how a microphone works.

The ________________ waves hit the diaphragm, which vibrates like your ________________.

The diaphragm, like the cells in your ________________, produces an electrical signal.

This signal carries the information to an amplifier and a loudspeaker.

Support

For Question **1b**, choose the descriptions from the following:

contains fluid (liquid) and hairs that produce an electrical signal
transfers (moves) the electrical signal to the brain
directs sound to the eardrum
directs sound to the auditory canal
vibrates and passes vibrations to the ossicles

For Question **3b**, use the following words to complete the sentences:

eardrum	sound	cochlea

2.5 Echoes and ultrasound

Investigating echoes

Learning objectives

- Explain how echoes are used to find distance
- Describe uses of ultrasound
- Compare sound and ultrasound

Task

1 Read the information your teacher gives you about echoes.

2 Answer the questions below.

Questions

Echoes

1 What is an echo?

____

2 a Give **one** example of where echoes can be useful.

____

b Give **one** example of where echoes are not useful.

____

3 a Explain why empty rooms produce lots of echoes.

____

____

b Explain why rooms with carpets and curtains do not usually produce lots of echoes.

____

____

Using echoes to calculate a distance

4 Name **two** uses of echoes.

____

____

5 Describe how bats and dolphins use ultrasound.

____

____

6 Describe how ultrasound can be used to determine how deep an ocean is.

____

____

Uses of ultrasound

7 Describe what ultrasound is.

____

____

8 Give **three** uses of ultrasound in medicine.

____

____

9 Describe how ultrasound can be used to create an image of an unborn baby.

____

____

____

____

Support

Using echoes to calculate a distance

For Question **6**, complete the sentences with the correct words.

A ____________ on a boat sends a pulse (beam) of ____________ towards the seabed.

The pulse is ____________ off the seabed.

A ____________ detects the pulse and uses the ____________ of ultrasound and the ____________ taken to receive the pulse to determine the depth of the seabed.

Uses of ultrasound

For Question **9**, complete the sentences with the correct words.

Ultrasound can be used to create an image of an unborn baby.

A ____________ sends pulses (beams) of ultrasound into a woman's stomach.

The ultrasound ____________ off the ____________ and a ____________ detects the reflected pulses.

A ____________ is used to build up an ____________ of the unborn baby from the ____________ pulse.

Practical: Transparent, translucent, and opaque

Learning objectives

- Describe the journey light takes
- Describe how the speed of light is used to define distance

Safety

- Be careful not to touch or put other materials near to the microscope lamp and ray box as they can become hot.
- Do not look directly into the light from the lamp.
- Take care with lifting and changing the direction of the lamps. They may get hot.

Equipment and materials

- light meter
- clamp stands
- cardboard to direct the torchlight
- light source
- materials to test, such as a beaker of water, different types of glass, tissue paper, greaseproof paper, a piece of opaque material such as metal foil or cloth

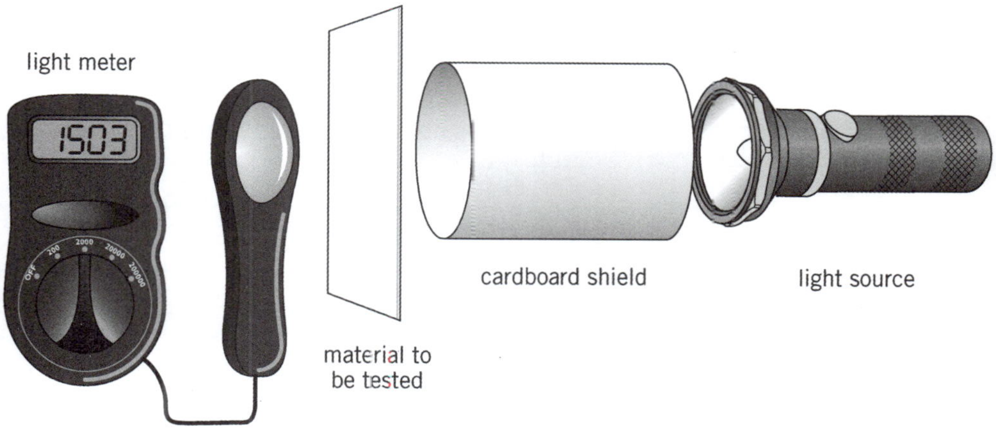

Method

You are going to test a number of different objects to determine which material will let the most light through.

1. Use the clamp stand to hold the light meter near the level of the bench.
2. Set up the light source 5–10 cm from the light meter, at the same height.
3. Make sure the light meter points towards the light source.
4. Arrange the cardboard to block out all light except the light from the light source.
5. Measure the light intensity with nothing between the light source and the light meter.
6. Record the reading in the table.
7. Put a material to be tested between the cardboard and the light meter.
8. Measure the light intensity and record the reading in your table.
9. Repeat steps **7** and **8** for each material and record the values as reading 1 in your table.
10. Repeat the experiment again with the same materials and record the results as reading 2 in your table.
11. Calculate the mean reading and record this in the last column.

Results

Material	Light intensity in lux		
	Reading 1	Reading 2	Mean light intensity

Questions

1 a Which material absorbed (took in) the most light? ______

b Which material transmitted (let through) the most light? ______

2 a Was your first set of readings the same as your second set of readings? ______

b If your second set of readings was not the same as your first set, explain why this may have happened.

______

______

c Were your results precise? How do you know?

______

______

3 For each word below, give an example from the materials that you tested and explain the meaning of the word.

Word	Example	Meaning
transparent		
translucent		
opaque		

4 A student sees a ball on the ground outside on a sunny day.

a Which object emits (gives out) the light? ______________________

b Which object reflects the light? ______________________

c What happens to the light when it hits your eye?

____

5 **a** Complete the sentences below about light-time.

Light-time is ______________ measured in terms of how far light travels in a given time.

A light-minute is the ______________ light travels in one ______________.

A light- ______________ is the ______________ light travels in one year.

b Why do scientists use light-time to measure distances in space instead of kilometres?

____

Support

For Question **3**, draw one line from each material to its meaning, and then one line from each meaning to an example. You can then fill in the table on page 172.

Material	Meaning	Example
transparent	a material that does not transmit light	a clear glass window
translucent	a see-through material that transmits most light	a piece of metal
opaque	a material that transmits light but it is scattered as it passes through	a frosted glass window

For Question **5a**, use the words below to help complete the sentences about light-time. You may need to use the words more than once, once, or not at all.

time	distance	large	Earth	minute	year

For Question **5b**, copy and complete the sentence below using **one** of the words from the list above.

Scientists use light-time to measure distances in space because the distances are very ______________.

3.2 Reflection

Practical: The law of reflection

Learning objectives

- Describe what happens when light is reflected
- Use the law of reflection to explain how images are formed in a plane mirror
- Describe the difference between specular reflection and diffuse reflection

Safety

- Take care when using the ray box as it can get very hot.
- Keep electrical equipment away from water.
- Do not look directly at light sources.

Equipment and materials

- ray box
- low-voltage power supply
- single slit
- plane (flat) mirror
- holders for mirror
- protractor
- white paper

Method

1. Place a mirror on its edge and draw a line along its edge.
2. Remove the mirror and draw a normal line to the centre of the mirror, at 90 ° to the mirror line.
3. Draw a line at 20 ° to the normal. This is the **angle of incidence**.
4. Place the mirror back onto its line and use the ray box to shine a ray of light along the line you drew in step **3**. This is the **incident ray**.
5. Mark the position of the **reflected ray** with small pencil dots.
6. Remove the equipment, join the dots up with a ruler, and measure the angle of reflection between the reflected ray and the normal.
7. Repeat steps **3–6** for angles of 30 °, 40 °, 50 °, and 60 °.
8. Record your results in the table.

Results

Angle of incidence in °	Angle of reflection in °
20	
30	
40	
50	
60	

Questions

1 **a** Which is the independent variable? ____________________

b Which is the dependent variable? ____________________

2 Describe the pattern in your results.

____

3 Suggest **one** way you could improve your experiment.

____

4 State the law of reflection.

____

5 Using the diagram match the part describing the ray diagram to the label.

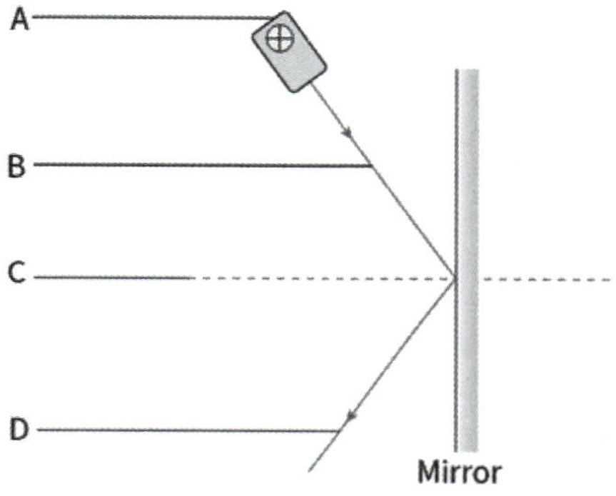

Part		Letter
1	incident ray	C
2	normal	A
3	ray box	D
4	reflected ray	B

6 Describe the difference between specular reflection and diffuse reflection. You may draw diagrams to help your description.

____

____

____

____

7 Use the law of reflection to explain how an image is formed in a plane mirror.

____

____

____

____

8 Describe **two** characteristics of the image seen in a plane mirror.

____

____

Support

Use this template to help carry out the practical. The mirror position and angles of incidence have been drawn for you. You need to draw the reflected rays onto it.

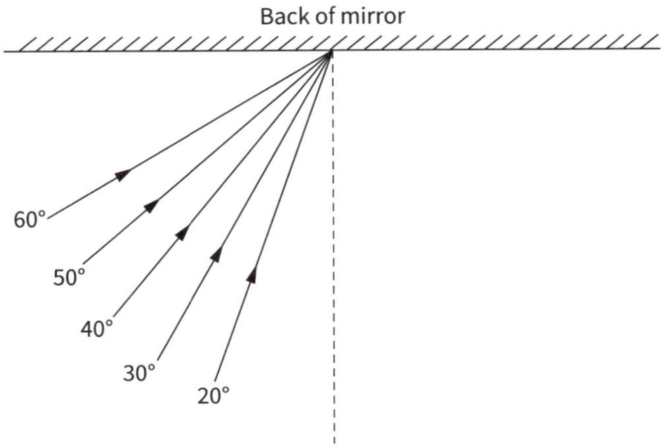

For Question **4**, complete this sentence:
The law of reflection states that:

the angle of ______________ is equal to the angle of ______________.

For Question **6**, complete the sentences using the words below. Each word can be used once or more than once.

one	light	different	reflected	smooth	rough

Specular reflection is when ______________ rays in one direction meet a ______________ surface and are all reflected in ______________ direction.

Diffuse scattering is when ______________ rays meet a ______________ surface and are ______________ in all ______________ directions.

For Question **7**, complete the sentences using the words below. Each word can be used once or more than once.

image	law	reflection	straight	reflected

When the light rays from the object are ______________ by the mirror, they obey the ______________ of ______________.

Our brain uses the fact that light travels in ______________ lines. If the reflected rays are extended as ______________ lines behind the mirror, they meet at a point and this is where the ______________ is formed.

3.3 Refraction

Practical: Investigating refraction

Learning objectives

- Explain what happens when light changes direction
- Describe how a convex lens affects light

Safety

- Take care when using the ray box as it can get very hot.
- Keep electrical equipment away from water.
- Do not look directly at light sources.

Equipment and materials

- ray box
- low-voltage power supply
- single slit
- rectangular glass block
- protractor
- white paper

Method

1 Place a glass block in the centre of a piece of white paper and draw around it.
2 Remove the glass block and draw a dotted normal line roughly in the middle of the boundary line, at right angles to the boundary line. Use a sharp pencil, a protractor, and a ruler.
3 Replace the glass block and use the ray box to shine a single ray of light along the normal line. Observe what happens to the ray.
4 Then use the ray box to shine a single ray of light at an angle towards one side of the glass block. This is the **incident ray**.
5 Mark the position of the incident ray with three small pencil dots.
6 Mark the position of the **refracted ray** that leaves the glass block with three small pencil dots.
7 Remove the glass block and join up each set of three dots.
8 Draw a line underneath where the glass block was, joining the ray coming in and the ray going out.
9 Draw a normal line at right angles to the block, at the point the refracted ray leaves the block.

Questions

1 Describe the path of the light through the block when it travels along the normal line.

____

2 Describe the path of the light as it travels at an angle:

from the air into the glass block: ______________________________

from the glass block into the air: ______________________________

PHYSICS

3 Describe what happens to the speed of the light ray at each boundary of the glass block.

air to glass: ______________________________

glass to air: ______________________________

4 Using the diagram match the part to the correct label that shows refraction.

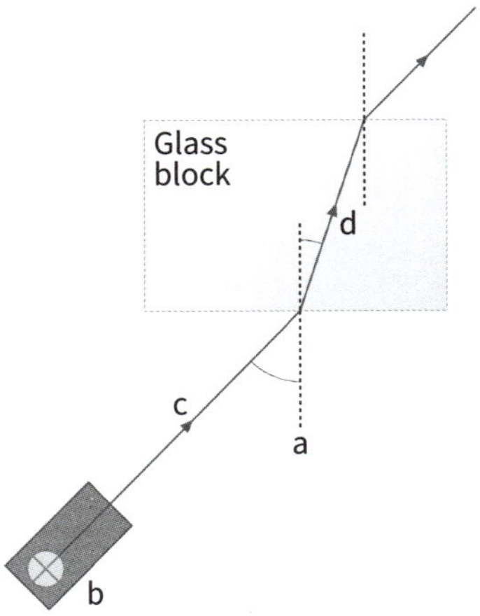

Part	**Label**
1 ray box	a
2 incident ray	b
3 normal	c
4 reflected ray	d

5 The diagram below shows light rays travelling towards a convex lens.
Complete the diagram to show what happens to the light rays after they pass through the lens.

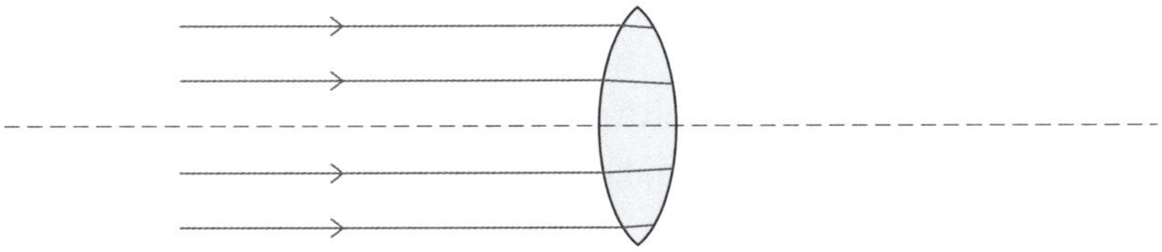

Support

For Questions **1** and **2**, choose the correct sentence to describe the path of the light in each case.

The light ray bends away from the normal.	The light ray does not change direction.	The light ray bends towards the normal.

For Question **3**, choose the correct sentence to describe what happens to the speed of the light ray at each boundary.

The light speeds up.	The light slows down.

3.4 The eye and the camera

Model making

Learning objectives

- Describe how the eye works
- Compare a simple camera with the eye

Safety

- Take care when using sharp objects (e.g. scissors).

Task

Use the information your teacher provides to carry out the tasks and answer the questions.

Questions

1 Label the diagram below to show the different parts of a camera viewing an object.

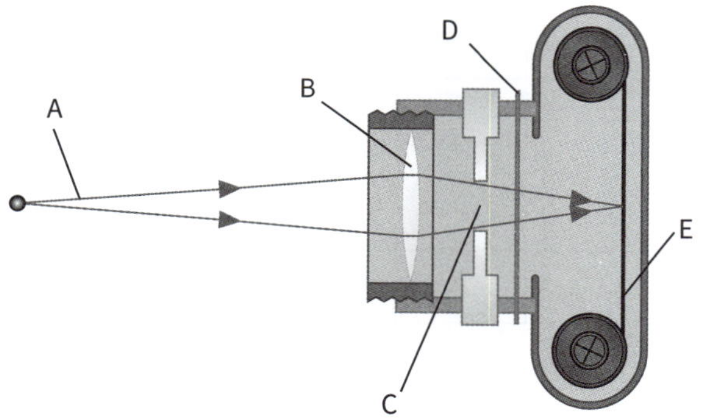

A ______________________________

B ______________________________

C ______________________________

D ______________________________

E ______________________________

2 Label the diagram below to show the different parts of an eye viewing an object.

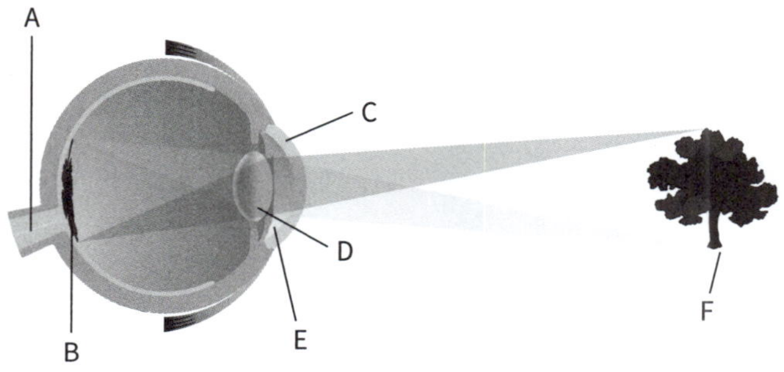

A ______________________________

B ______________________________

C ______________________________

D ______________________________

E ______________________________

F ______________________________

3 Your teacher will give you some materials from which to make a model.

- Choose materials to represent each part of the eye.
- Make a model of the eye using these items.
- Repeat the steps above to make a model of a camera.
- On your diagrams, add the materials you have chosen for each part of the eye and for each part of the camera.

4 List parts of the eye that are **also** in the camera.

____

5 Describe how the eye works to form an image that is sent to the brain.

____

____

____

____

Support

For Question **1**, use these key words to label the camera diagram.

lens	photographic film	aperture
shutter	ray	

For Question **2**, use these key words to label the eye diagram.

lens	pupil	object	cornea	optic nerve	retina

For Question **5**, use these key words in your answer.

lens	retina	real	inverted	image	photoreceptors	electrical impulse	brain

3.5 Colour

Practical: Investigating colour

Learning objectives

- Describe what happens when light passes through a prism
- Understand how primary colours make secondary colours
- Explain the effect of filters and coloured materials on light

Safety

- Act sensibly when working in a darkened room.
- Do not look directly into the light from the lamp.

Equipment and materials

- A4 plain white paper
- red, blue, and green lights
- red, blue, and green filters
- red, blue, and green shapes
- black paper
- white paper

Tasks and questions

White light

1 Your teacher will show you how white light can be split (divided) up.

a Describe what happens when white light passes through a glass prism.

____

____

b Explain why this happens.

____

____

Combining colours

2 Your teacher will show you how colours can be combined. Record your predictions and results in the table.

a Predict which colour of light is produced when different colours of light are mixed together.

b Complete the table with the actual (true) colour produced. State if it is a secondary or a tertiary colour.

Primary colours of light mixed	Predicted colour produced	Actual colour produced	Secondary or tertiary colour
red and green			
red and blue			
red and green			
red, blue, and green			

Filters

3 You will now investigate which colour lights can pass through different filters.

a Predict the colour of red light after it passes through a red filter. Write your prediction in the results table below.

b Shine red light through a red filter onto white paper. Record the colour you see in the table.

c Repeat steps **a** and **b** for each colour of light and filter.

d Use your results to suggest a rule to predict which colour of light passes through a coloured filter.

____

____

		Colour of light after it passes through filter	
Colour of light	**Colour of filter**	**Predicted**	**Actual**
red	red		
blue	red		
green	red		
red	blue		
blue	blue		
green	blue		
red	green		
blue	green		
green	green		

Coloured objects

4 You will now investigate what colour different coloured objects look in different colours of light.

a Predict the appearance of each coloured object in different coloured light. Write your predictions in the results table on the next page.

b Place the red object onto black paper and shine red light onto it.

c Record the actual colour that the object looks in the table.

d Repeat steps **b** and **c** for each colour of light and colour of object, and record your results.

e Explain why a blue jumper looks blue in white light.

____

____

f What colour will a red hat look in blue light? Explain your answer.

____

____

g Use your results to suggest a rule to predict what colour an object appears in different colours of light.

____

____

____

____

Colour of light	True colour of object	Appearance of object in coloured light	
		Predicted	Actual
red	red		
blue	red		
green	red		
red	blue		
blue	blue		
green	blue		
red	green		
blue	green		
green	green		

Support

For Question **1a**, use these key words and phrases in your answer.

refracts	disperses	continuous spectrum

For Question **1b**, use these key words in your answer.

frequencies	colours

For Question **3d**, copy and complete the sentences below.

A coloured filter only lets ________________ pass through if it is the same colour as the filter.

All other colours of light are ________________ by the filter.

For Question **4e**, use these key words in your answer.

reflects	absorbs

For Question **4f**, use these key words in your answer.

reflects	absorbs

For Question **4g**, copy and complete the sentences below by choosing the correct word from the words in **bold**.

If a coloured object is not the same colour as the light shining on it, the object will appear to be **black / white**.
If the object is the same colour as the light, the object will appear to be **a different colour from / the same colour as** the coloured light.

4.1 Speed

Calculating speed

Learning objectives

- Calculate average speed
- Describe the difference between average and instantaneous speed
- Describe examples of relative motion

Task

Working in pairs, you are going to measure your average speed across different activities.

Equipment

- tape measure
- stopwatch

Method

1 Mark out a distance of at least 5 m.
2 Walk the distance while your partner uses a stopwatch to time how long it takes.
3 Record the time in a results table and repeat the measurement.
4 Calculate your average time.
5 Calculate your average speed by dividing the distance walked by the average time.

$$\text{average speed (m/s)} = \frac{\text{total distance (m)}}{\text{total time taken (s)}}$$

6 Repeat steps **2–5** for different activities, such as skipping or hopping.

Results

Record your results in the table below.

Activity	Time in s			Speed in m/s
	1	2	Average	
walking				

Questions

1 **a** Results are *precise* when the repeats are very similar to each other and the average value.
Look at your results and decide if they are precise results.

b Results are *accurate* if they are close to the true value.
Describe how you measured the distance and time to make sure your results were accurate.

2 A student runs 240 m in 40 s. Calculate their average speed.

3 Ospreys fly from Africa to the UK in the summer. They can fly 275 kilometres in 5 hours and 30 minutes. Calculate the average speed of the osprey.

4 A train is moving north at 90 km/h. A second train travels south on a parallel track at a speed of 50 km/h. Describe the relative motion of the trains.

5 A runner is running at 8 m/s when a second runner moving at 9 m/s in the same direction passes them. Describe the relative motion of the two runners.

Support

When completing your results table, remember:

$$\text{average time} = \frac{(\text{time 1} + \text{time 2})}{2}$$

For Question **1a**, choose the correct words in **bold** to complete the sentences.

When I repeated the measurement for the walking activity, the repeat was **similar to / different from** the first value.

This means my results for the activity are **precise / not precise**.

For Question **1b**, choose the correct words to complete the sentences.

Distance

I used a ______________________________

To make sure I measured the distance accurately, I ______________________________

____

Time

I used a ______________________________

To make sure I timed accurately, I ______________________________

____

For Questions **2** and **3**, use this equation:

$$\text{average speed (m/s)} = \frac{\text{total distance (m)}}{\text{total time taken (s)}}$$

4.2 Motion graphs

Plotting motion graphs

Learning objectives

- Interpret a distance–time graph
- Use data from a distance–time graph to calculate average speed

Questions

The table below shows the distance–time data for a bus journey.

Time in s	Distance travelled in metres
0	0
30	240
70	820
190	820
310	1300
400	1400

1 Plot the distance–time graph for the bus journey on the axes below.
The first 30 seconds have been plotted for you.

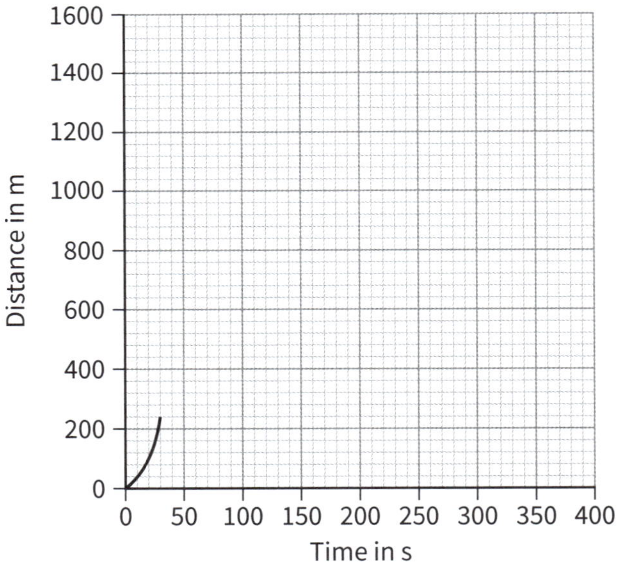

2 Label the sections on the graph where the bus is:
- moving at the slowest constant (steady) speed
- accelerating
- not moving
- moving at the fastest constant speed.

3 Calculate the average speed for the whole journey.

____

____

4 Calculate the average speed for the first 200 s of the bus journey.

____

____

5 Calculate the average speed from 200 s to 400 s.

____

____

Support

For Question **1**, use the axes below to plot the graph. The first 70 seconds have been plotted for you.

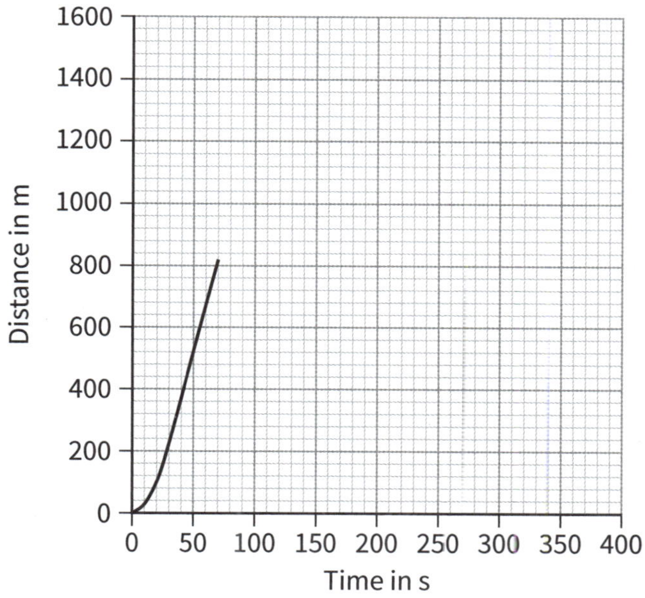

For Question **3**, copy and complete these steps of the calculation:

time = 400 s
distance = ______________________ m

$$\text{average speed (m/s)} = \frac{\text{distance (m)}}{\text{time (s)}}$$

$$= \frac{\square}{\square}$$

$$= \square \text{ m/s}$$

For Question **4**, copy and complete these steps of the calculation:

time = 200 s
distance at 200 s = ______________________ m

$$\text{average speed (m/s)} = \frac{\text{distance (m)}}{\text{time (s)}}$$

$$= \frac{\square}{\square}$$

$$= \square \text{ m/s}$$

For Question **5**, copy and complete these steps of the calculation:

time = 200 s
distance = 1400 − ________________ = ________________ m

$$\text{average speed (m/s)} = \frac{\text{distance (m)}}{\text{time (s)}}$$

$$= \frac{\square}{\square}$$

$$= \square \text{ m/s}$$

4.3 Pressure in gases

Observing pressure in gases

Learning objectives

- Describe how volume and temperature affect gas pressure
- Describe atmospheric pressure
- Describe how atmospheric pressure changes with height

Task

Watch your teacher carry out several experiments. Write your observations for each one below. You can also add labelled diagrams.

Collapsing bottle

Describe what your teacher did to the bottle.

____

____

____

Describe what happened when the bottle cooled down.

____

____

____

Unspillable water

What happened when the glass was turned upside down?

____

____

____

Expanding marshmallows

Describe the marshmallows at the start.

____

____

____

Describe what your teacher did.

Describe the marshmallows at the end.

Two balloons

Describe the balloons before one was put in the freezer.

Describe the balloons now.

Balloon in a syringe

Describe what happens to the balloon when the plunger is pushed and the opening is clear.

Describe what happens to the balloon when the plunger is pushed and the opening is covered.

Questions

1 State what causes atmospheric pressure.

____

2 Describe the change in atmospheric pressure as altitude (height) increases.

____

3 Describe what happens to gas pressure when the temperature changes.

____

____

4 Describe what happens to gas pressure when the volume changes.

____

____

5 Describe what happened in the collapsing bottle experiment. Consider the points below in your answer:

- the cause of pressure *inside* the bottle
- the cause of pressure *outside* the bottle
- the difference in pressure inside the bottle between heating and cooling.

____

____

____

____

____

Support

For Question **3**, copy and complete this sentence:

When the temperature of a gas increases, the gas pressure ______________________________.

For Question **4**, copy and complete this sentence:

When the volume of a gas decreases, the gas pressure ______________________________.

For Question **5**, copy and complete this paragraph:

To start, the bottle is heated.
The air molecules inside the bottle ______________ with the inside of the bottle, exerting gas ______________.
When the bottle is removed from the water bath, the temperature inside the bottle ______________, so there are ______________ collisions (hits) between the molecules and the inside of the bottle.

As a result, the gas pressure inside the bottle becomes ______________ than the atmospheric pressure outside the bottle, which causes the bottle to ______________.

4.4 Pressure in liquids

Floating and sinking

Learning objectives

- Describe how liquids exert a pressure in all directions
- Describe how liquid pressure changes with depth
- Explain why some everyday objects float and some sink

Questions

1 When a submarine is underwater, there is a pressure acting on it.
Describe how a liquid exerts (applies) a pressure.

2 Describe how liquid pressure changes with depth.

3 Two bottles are filled with water. The diagram below shows how the water flows from a hole halfway down the bottle.

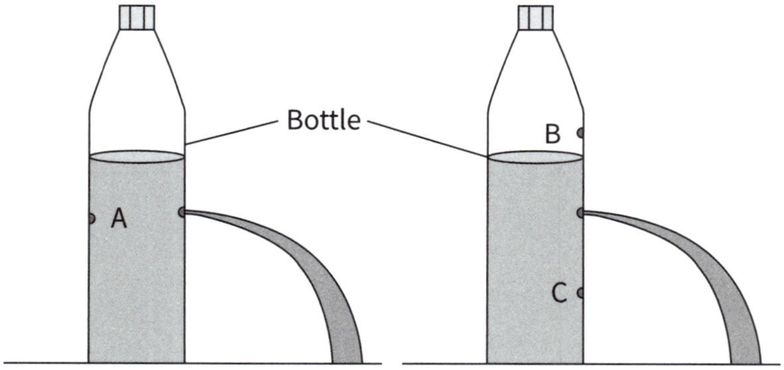

Complete the diagram to show how the water flows from holes **A**, **B**, and **C**.

Task

Your teacher will give you a lump of modelling clay.

Investigate which shapes will float (stay on the surface of the water) and which will sink (move down below the surface of the water).

Record your observations in the results table.

Results

Shape of modelling clay	Observations

Conclusion

Write a conclusion to your investigation, explaining why some shapes of modelling clay float. Use these key words:

pressure	upthrust	area	weight

____

____

____

____

____

Support

For Question **1**, choose the correct words to complete this paragraph:

When a submarine is underwater, there is a ______________ acting on it due to the water molecules.

This is because of the ______________ of the water ______________ on the surface of the submarine.

The pressure is exerted (applied) in ______________ directions.

For Question **2**, choose the correct word to complete this sentence:

As you go deeper in a liquid, the pressure ______________.

For the **conclusion**, choose the correct key words below to complete the paragraph. You may use some words more than once.

pressure	upthrust	area	weight	float

Increasing the ______________ of the bottom of the clay allowed the clay to ______________.

This is because it increased the ______________ acting on the clay.

When the ______________ was equal to the ______________, the clay floated (stayed on the surface of the water).

It is water ______________ that produces the ______________.

4.5 Pressure on solids

Investigating pressure on solids

Learning objectives

- Describe pressure on a solid, and give the direction that it acts in
- Calculate pressure
- Describe situations where high or low pressures are useful

Task

You are going to plan an investigation to answer this question:

Is the pressure exerted on the ground greater when you stand on one foot than when you stand on two feet?

Equipment

- squared paper
- scales (measuring newtons)

Prediction

I think when you stand on one foot the pressure will be:

____

This is because:

____

Plan

To investigate, I will:

____

____

____

____

____

Questions

1 One student carried out an investigation and collected the data below :
- weight = 650 N
- area of one foot = 0.0104 m^2

a Calculate the pressure exerted when the student stands on one foot.

b Calculate the pressure exerted when the student stands on both feet.

c Use your answers to parts **a** and **b** to write a conclusion:
Is the pressure exerted on the ground greater when you stand on one foot than when you stand on two feet?

2 Write down the definition of *pressure*.

3 Explain why rucksacks are designed with wide straps.

4 Describe the difference between a blunt knife and a sharp knife.

Support

For the **Prediction**, choose the correct word in **bold** to complete the first sentence. Then complete the second sentence with a reason.

I think when you stand on one foot the pressure will be **the same / greater / smaller**.

This is because ______________________________

For the **Plan**, choose the correct words to complete the sentence.

To investigate, I will measure my weight using the ______________________________ and I will measure the area of my foot by ______________________________

For Questions **1a** and **1b**, use the information below:

$$\text{pressure (N/m}^2\text{)} = \frac{\text{force (N)}}{\text{area (m}^2\text{)}}$$

area of two feet = $2 \times 0.0104\text{m}^2$

For Question **1c**, choose the correct words in **bold** to complete the sentences.

When you stand on one foot, the pressure is **the same / greater / smaller**.

This is because **the same / a bigger / a smaller** force is acting over **the same / a greater / a smaller** area.

For Question **3**, choose the correct words to complete the sentences.

The wide straps ______________________________ the area in contact with the body.

The ______________________________ acts over a ______________________________ area.

This ______________________________ the pressure.

For Question **4**, remember:

A *sharp knife* will have a *smaller area*.

Practical: Measuring moments

Learning objectives

- Define the moment of a force
- Calculate the moment of a force
- Apply the law of moments

Safety

- Take care so that masses do not fall.

Equipment and materials

- ruler
- triangular pivot
- masses

Method

1 Rest the ruler on the triangular pivot. Balance the ruler so that it is horizontal.
2 Add two masses to one side of the ruler near to the pivot.
3 Place a single mass on the opposite side of the ruler as shown in the diagram below.

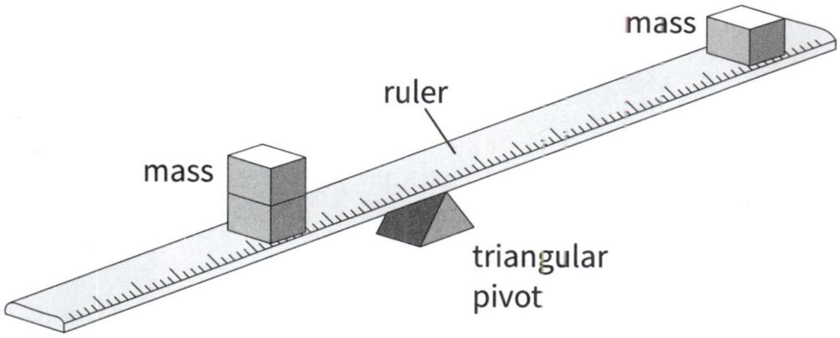

4 Move the single mass until the ruler is balanced.
5 Record the weight of the masses and their distances from the pivot in the results table.
6 Calculate the clockwise (to the right) and anticlockwise (to the left) moments.
7 Repeat with different masses. Try to identify a pattern in your results.

Results

Left-hand side of the ruler		Right-hand side of the ruler			
Force in N	Distance from the centre of the mass to the pivot in cm	Anticlockwise moment	Force in N	Distance from the centre of the mass to the pivot in cm	Clockwise moment

Questions

1 Describe the relationship between the clockwise moment and the anticlockwise moment when the ruler T is balanced.

2 The diagram below shows a plank of wood being used to lift a large stone.

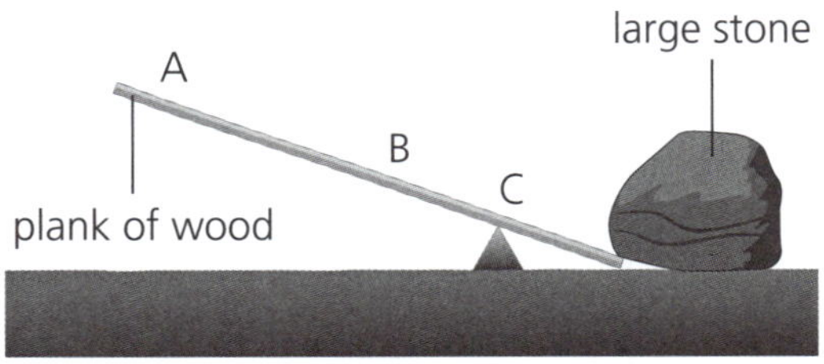

State whether you would push down at **A**, **B**, or **C**. Explain your decision.

3 A child weighs 600 N and sits 2 m from the pivot of a seesaw. Calculate the moment of the child.

4 The diagram below shows a tractor driving along a slope.

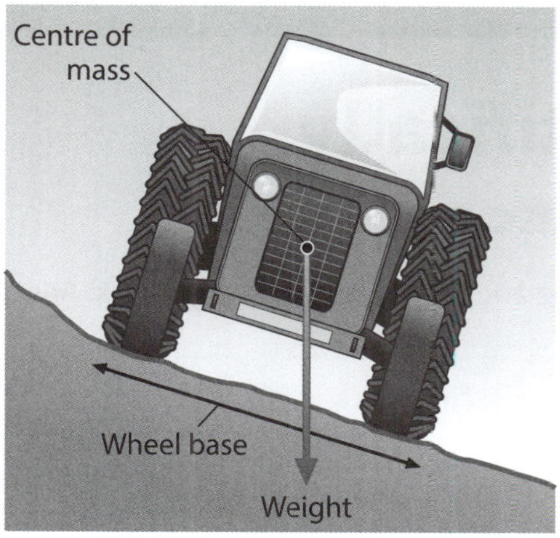

Explain why it is dangerous for a tractor to drive on the side of a steep slope.

____

____

____

Support

For Question **1**, choose the correct word to complete this sentence:

When the ruler is balanced, the clockwise (to the right) moment ____________ the anticlockwise (to the left) moment.

For Question **2**, choose the correct words to complete these sentences:

I would push down at ____________ because it is ____________ the pivot.

This would give me the largest ____________ for the same ____________ applied.

For Question **3**, complete these calculations:

moment (Nm) = force (N) × distance (m) = ____________ × ____________

moment = ____________ Nm

For Question **4**, choose the correct words to complete these sentences:

If the slope is very steep, the ____________ might act outside of the base.

This would cause the tractor to ____________.

Answers

Working scientifically

WS1.1 Asking scientific questions

Answers depend on the items available and the questions that you ask. Another example is given in the Support section.

For the example of a toy car:

Idea: Can the toy car travel far?

Scientific question: How far does a toy car move when it rolls down ramps of different heights?

Independent variable: vertical height of the ramp

Dependent variable: distance from end of the ramp

Control variables: length of ramp, mass of car, material of ramp, type of tyres

WS1.2 Working safely

1 1 (barrel (tube)) – A, 2 (air hole) – B, 3 (base) – E, 4 (collar (band)) – C, 5 (gas hose) – D

2 any **one** from: base (E), collar (band) (C), gas hose (D)

3 **a** closed; when you are not heating anything – the safety flame

b open in part; to heat substances up gently – the gentle flame

c completely open; to heat substances strongly – the roaring flame

WS1.3 Planning investigations

The following are example answers.

1 a suitable 2D image of a measuring cylinder, drawn with a ruler and pencil

2 I poured the liquid into a measuring cylinder and looked directly across at the scale to read the volume, taking the reading from the base of the meniscus.

3 I lined the 0 on the ruler up with the bottom of the pile, then read the ruler at the top of the pile. (The 0 needs to line up with the bottom of the pile, not the bottom of the ruler. There is often a gap between 0 and the bottom of the ruler.)

4 I used a balance because it is able to measure an object with a very small mass. Bathroom scales would not be able to register a reading / they would be less accurate / they are designed to measure larger masses.

5 paper rolled up into different sized balls / different surface area of balls / not measuring the height dropped accurately / human error with stopwatch / different types of paper, etc.

WS1.4 Recording data

1 type of ball
2 height of bounce of ball in cm
3 any **two** from: initial height of ball drop in cm, temperature of ball, type of surface the ball is dropped on
4

Type of ball	Bounce height in cm			
	First reading	Second reading	Third reading	Mean bounce height in cm

5 correct means calculated and added to table
6 answer based on results

Support

1 The **independent** variable is **type of ball**.
2 The **dependent** variable height of bounce (in cm).
3 A **control variable** is height it falls.
4

Type of ball	Bounce height in cm			
	First reading	Second reading	Third reading	Mean bounce height in cm

WS1.5 Presenting data

correct graphs and charts drawn

WS1.6 Analysing data

Graph: Perfect straight-line graph through the origin.

Conclusion: As the volume of water increases, the height of water increases.

WS1.7 Evaluating data

Experiment 1	Experiment 2
some balls bounced, others thrown before hitting	all balls thrown before hitting
	same hitting force used each time
stood in different places	all balls hit from same point
no measurements taken	measurements taken with measuring tape
only tennis balls repeated	all results repeated three times
	mean distance travelled calculated

1 Experiment 2; better scientific method – see table above

2 any **three** improvements to Experiment 1 from: throw all balls before hitting, use same force each time, take all results from same point, take measurements, repeat all results three times, calculate a mean distance travelled

B1 Cells

B1.1 Observing cells

1 Order of labels for the microscope (top to bottom, left side): objective lens – lens you choose to magnify the image; stage clips – hold microscope slide in place; light source – provides light to see the image.

Order of labels for the microscope (top to bottom, right side): eyepiece lens – lens you look through, magnifies the image; stage – platform for object or slide being looked at; coarse focus – nearly focuses the image; fine focus – focuses the object in sharp detail; base – stops the microscope from moving.

2 Your own drawing of one object

3 Your own calculation of total magnification

B1.2 Plant and animal cells

1 and 2

Part	Seen in an onion cell	Seen in a cheek cell	Function (job)
cell membrane	✓	✓	controls what enters and leaves a cell
cell wall	✓	✓	makes the cell stronger and provides support
nucleus	✓	✓	controls the cell and contains genetic material
cytoplasm	✓	✓	'jelly-like' substance where chemical reactions occur
mitochondria	✓	✓	where respiration occurs
vacuole	✓	✓	contains cell sap and keeps the cell firm

3 Chloroplasts/Chlorophyll absorb (take in) light energy from the Sun for photosynthesis. Onion cells are found underground where there is no light.

B1.3 Specialized cells

Specialized cell	Plant or animal?	Function (job)	Diagram	Adaptations	Challenge: How do the adaptations allow it to perform its function?
nerve cell	animal	carry electrical impulses around the body		long and thin, connections at each end	carry impulses over long distances, join to other nerve cells/ muscles or glands to cause an effect
red blood cell	animal	transport oxygen		contains haemoglobin, no nucleus, curves in on both sides	haemoglobin joins to oxygen, large surface area for carrying oxygen
skeletal muscle cell	animal	contracts to cause movement	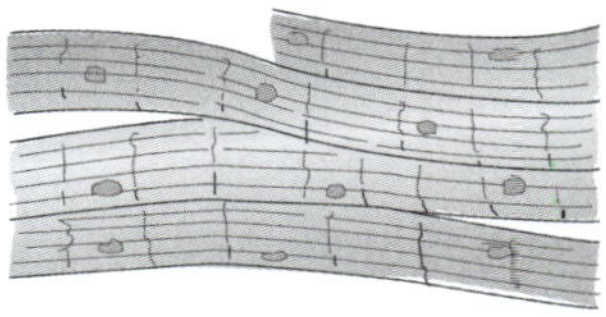	many mitochondria, protein filaments	mitochondria transfer energy to the cell, protein filaments slide past each other to shorten the cell
leaf cell	plant	photosynthesis	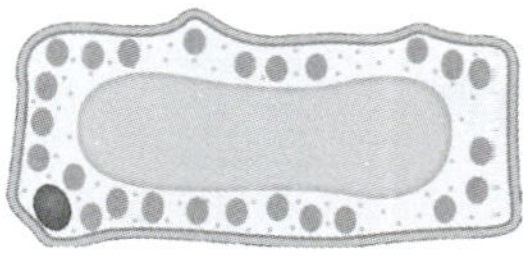	long and thin, packed with chloroplasts	large surface area for taking in energy from the Sun
root hair cell	plant	take in water/ nutrients	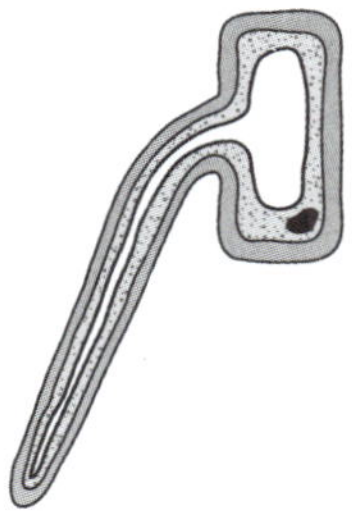	large surface area, no chloroplasts	large surface area to take in water and nutrients

B1.4 Movement of substances

1 The water becomes more coloured over time. The dye spreads out into the water.
2 The gel does not change / is not dissolved. The gel becomes paler in colour.
3 Diffusion has occurred. The dye molecules move from a high concentration (strength) in the gel to a low concentration in the water. (In the water, the dye then moves from high concentration [by the gel] to a lower concentration [throughout the water].)

Support gap-fill conclusion:

gel, water, spreads, diffusion

B1.5 Unicellular organisms

1

Found in amoeba	Found in euglenas	Found in both
food vacuole	chloroplasts	nucleus
pseudopod	flagellum	cell membrane
	eye spot	cytoplasm
		contractile vacuole

2 Shape of the cell / amoeba is bigger / euglena appears green.
3 Amoeba because it is bigger / slower moving.
4 By dividing itself into two (identical) cells. This is known as binary fission.

B2 Body systems

B2.1 Levels of organization

Task 1

1 cells
2 nucleus, cytoplasm, cell membrane
3 any three from: muscle cell, nerve cell, ciliated epithelial cell, sperm cell, red blood cell, root hair cell, fat cell, egg cell
4 A group of similar cells working together to carry out a function (job).
5 organ
6 A group of organs working together to carry out a function.

Task 2

For example:

Organ system	Main functions (jobs)	Organs found in the system
circulatory system	transports blood around the body; delivers oxygen and nutrients to cells and takes away waste	heart, veins, arteries

Support

1 tissue – group of cells working together
organ system – group of organs working together
organ – group of tissues working together
2 cell ⟶ organ ⟶ organ system ⟶ tissue
3 any two from: muscle cell, nerve cell, ciliated epithelial cell, sperm cell, red blood cell, root hair cell, fat cell, egg cell
4 skeleton/skeletal system; respiratory system; digestive system

B2.2 Skeleton

Task 1

1 A – skull; B – vertebrae; C – clavicle; D – humerus; E – ribs; F – radius and ulna; G – pelvis; H – wrist bones; I – femur; J – tibia and fibula; K – ankle bones

Questions

1 ribs/ribcage; skull; vertebrae; ribs/ribcage
2 any two from: support, movement, making blood
3 any two from: hard outer layer, soft tissue centre, blood supply

Support

1 A – skull; B – vertebrae; C – clavicle; D – humerus; E – ribs; F – radius and ulna; G – pelvis; H – wrist bones; I – femur; J – tibia and fibula; K – ankle bones
2 The skeleton **supports** the body and holds your organs in place.
It **protects** important organs like the brain.
The skeleton helps the body to **move**.
Some bones also make **blood** cells.

B2.3 Movement: joints

Questions

1 Your strongest muscle.
2 A – bone (kneecap); B – fluid/liquid; C – cartilage; D – ligament
3 ligament – joins two bones together
cartilage – covers the end of the bone
fluid (liquid) – keeps the joint slippery so bones do not rub together

Support

1 Completed table.
2 bone – A; ligament – D; fluid (liquid) – B; cartilage – C
3 ligament – joins two bones together
cartilage – covers the end of the bone
fluid (liquid) – keeps the joint slippery so bones do not rub together

B2.4 Movement: muscles

Questions

1 card – bone; split pin – joint; string 1 – triceps muscle; string 2 – biceps muscle; coloured section of string – tendon

2 The muscle contracts, pulling on a bone.

3 When one muscle contracts, the other muscle relaxes to cause movement.

To move in the opposite direction, the muscle that contracted must relax, and the muscle that relaxed must contract.

4 straight arm: triceps contracted, biceps relaxed
bent arm: triceps relaxed, biceps contracted

Support

1 You should have added the following labels to the diagram:
muscle: pointing to the two black lines/strings

bone: pointing to the main parts of the model

joint: pointing to the black dot where the upper part of the model joins the lower part

2 The muscle **contracts, pulling** on a bone.

3 When one muscle contracts (gets shorter), the mother muscle **relaxe**s to cause movement.

To move in the opposite direction, the muscle that contracted must **relax**, and the muscle that relaxed must **contract**.

B2.5 Breathing: lungs

Questions

1 Answers will depend on your calculated lung volume and number of breaths per minute.
Answers using the values in the support are:
Student A: $21 \times 420 = 8820\ cm^3$
Student B: $19 \times 510 = 9690\ cm^3$
Student C: $18 \times 380 = 6840\ cm^3$

2 The muscles between your ribs relax. This pulls your ribcage down and in. The diaphragm relaxes, so it moves up. Air is forced out of your lungs.

B2.6 Breathing: gas exchange

Task 1

1 A – nose; B – mouth; C – trachea; D – ribcage; E – intercostal muscle; F – heart; G – lung; H – bronchus; I – bronchiole; J – alveolus; K – rib; L – diaphragm

2 Ribs – hard and strong (to protect the lungs).
Alveoli – have a large surface area and thin walls (one cell thick). (This means that gas exchange can occur quickly and easily.)

Task 2

Two bar charts, correctly drawn.

Questions

1 alveolus (alveoli)
2 carbon dioxide
3 nitrogen
4 21 − 16 = 5%
5 It is used in the body during respiration.
6 No, we also breathe out other gases, including oxygen and nitrogen.

B2.7 Aerobic respiration

Task 1

1 glucose + oxygen ⟶ carbon dioxide + water + energy
2 Completed table as follows:

Product	Chemical used	Positive result
carbon dioxide	limewater	turns from clear to cloudy
water	cobalt chloride paper	turns from blue to pink

Task 2

1 The muscles between your ribs relax. This pulls your ribcage **down** and **in**. The diaphragm relaxes, so it moves **up**. Air is forced **out** of your lungs.

Questions

1 in the mitochondria
2 plasma
3 Oxygen is brought into the lungs when we breathe in. In the alveoli, oxygen diffuses from the lungs to the blood. Then the oxygen binds with haemoglobin in the red blood cells and is carried to cells in the bloodstream.

Support

- **Oxygen** is taken in when you breathe in. It diffuses into the blood in your **lungs/alveoli**.
- **Oxygen** is carried by the **red blood** cells. It then diffuses into the cell that needs it.
- During digestion, carbohydrates are broken down into **glucose**. This is absorbed (taken) into the blood in the **small intestine**.
- **Glucose** dissolves in the **blood/plasma** and is carried to the cell that needs it.
- Respiration occurs inside the **mitochondria** within a cell.
- The gas **carbon dioxide** is produced. This dissolves in the blood **plasma**.
- It diffuses into the air sacs in the **lungs** and is realised from the body when you breathe.
- **Water** is also produced by aerobic respiration.

B2.8 Anaerobic respiration

Questions

1 Completed table as follows:

	Aerobic respiration	Anaerobic respiration	Fermentation
Glucose is a reactant.	✓	✓	✓
Oxygen is a reactant.	✓		
Carbon dioxide is produced.	✓		✓
Ethanol is produced.			✓
Lactic acid is produced.		✓	
Water is produced.	✓		

2 glucose $\rightarrow$ lactic acid (+ energy)

3 Aerobic respiration releases more energy per glucose molecule than anaerobic respiration.
Aerobic respiration does not lead to lactic acid build-up / cramp.

B3 Health and lifestyle

B3.1 Nutrients

Task 1

Part	Function(s) in the body	Example
carbohydrates	provide energy	pasta / bread
lipids	provide energy / keep you warm / protect organs	butter / cheese / vegetable oil
proteins	growth and repair	fish / chicken / eggs
vitamins	keep you healthy	fruits / vegetables
minerals	keep you healthy	milk / fruits / vegetables
water	needed in all cells and body fluids	water / tea / juice
fibre	provides bulk (roughage) to food to keep it moving through the gut (your digestive system)	vegetables / wholewheat pasta / brown rice

Question

1 a diet that provides the right/correct nutrients in the right/correct amounts

Support

1 1 carbohydrates – **C**. provide energy
2 lipids – **G**. provide energy / keep you warm / protect organs
3 proteins – **F**. growth and repair
4 vitamins – **B**./**E**. keep you healthy
5 minerals – **B**./**E**. keep you healthy
6 water – **A**. needed in all cells and body fluids
7 fibre – **D**. provides bulk (roughage) to food to keep it moving through the gut (digestive system) a diet that provides the right (correct) **nutrients** in the right/correct **amounts**

B3.2 Digestive system

Plan

Your plan should show the position of the main structures in the digestive system (i.e. mouth, gullet, stomach, small intestine, large intestine, rectum, anus). You should state the material that you are going to use to represent each organ, and add the information that you are going to include on the description label.

Evaluation

You should include at least one positive feature and one negative feature of your model.

Positive features could include:

- shows the position of the organs in the digestive system
- shows the order of the structures the food passes through in the digestive system
- shows some differences in organ structure.

Negative features could include:

- movement of liquid relies on gravity – does not show peristalsis (muscles pushing food along)
- detailed internal structure of organs may not be seen – for example, villi in small intestine
- does not show absorption/enzymes being added.

Support

1 **1** rectum – **E**
   2 small intestine – **C**
   3 stomach – **B**
   4 large intestine – **D**
   5 gullet – **A**
   6 anus – **F**

2 Own choices of materials.

3 **1** rectum – **B**. Faeces (waste) are stored here until they leave the body.
   2 gullet – **A**. Food passes down this tube.
   3 stomach – **E**. Food is mixed with digestive juices and acids.
   4 small intestine – **D**. Small molecules of nutrients pass through the intestine wall into the blood.
   5 large intestine – **C**. Water passes back into the body and faeces are formed.

B3.3 Food tests

Task

Food group	Chemical	Positive result
starch	iodine	blue–black
sugar	Benedict's solution	orange–red
fat	ethanol	cloudy
protein	biuret solution	purple

Questions

1 Answer will depend on results. Make sure you have identified the correct change for each food group.

2 Answer will depend on results. Make sure you have identified the correct change for each food group.

3 Answer will depend on results. You should select a food that contains fat and/or sugar, as only a little of these should be eaten in a balanced diet.

B3.4 Unhealthy diet

Questions

1 male construction worker
2 9000 kJ
3 2000 kJ
4 D
5 57.1%

Support

1 male officer worker = 12 000 kJ; female office worker = 10 000 kJ; difference = 2000 kJ

B3.5 Bacteria and enzymes in digestion

Hypothesis

When **an enzyme** (carbohydrase) is added to **starch** (a carbohydrate), it will break the **starch** down. Eventually, it will be completely broken down into smaller parts. This is because **enzymes** are biological catalysts. They **speed up** reactions without being used up.

Prediction

I am going to investigate this by adding **carbohydrase** to a starch solution. I will then add this to **iodine** at different time intervals.

I predict that, over time, the starch and carbohydrase solution will **stop** turning the iodine blue–black. This is because iodine is a test for **starch**, and the **carbohydrase** will have broken down the **starch**.

Questions

1 At 0 minutes, the iodine solution turned from orange to blue–black when solution A was added. The same happened at each one-minute interval when solution A was added.
2 At 0 minutes, the iodine solution turned from orange to blue–black when solution B was added. You should note that after a certain number of minutes, the colour did not change (for each new well in the row on the spotting tile).
3 This is time in minutes until the iodine solution did not change colour
4 If the experiment is carried out correctly, you should conclude that your results do support your hypothesis and that your prediction was correct. Reasons given include: solution A had no enzyme in it. This means the starch did not break down, so the iodine changed colour as there was starch in the solution. Solution B contained the enzyme carbohydrase. After a certain number of minutes, the colour did not change because the starch had been broken down into sugar. (Iodine does not test for sugar.)

Support

All of the results in row A showed a colour change from orange to blue–black. This is because **starch** was present in all of these results.

In row B, there was no colour change after **your time** minutes. This showed when the starch had been digested into **sugar**.

B3.6 Harmful substances

Task 1: The harmful effects of smoking

1 thermometer; cigarette; cotton wool; limewater; universal indicator solution

2 thermometer – to measure temperature change; cotton wool – to represent lung tissue; limewater – to test for carbon dioxide (but remember that tobacco smoke also contains carbon monoxide); universal indicator solution – to test for acidity level

3 Likely observations:

	Before	Fresh air	Cigarette smoke
Temperature in °C	room temperature	room temperature	higher than room temperature
Colour of cotton wool	white	white	yellow/brown
Colour of universal indicator solution	green	green	yellow/orange
Colour of limewater	clear	clear	cloudy

Questions

1 tar

2 It narrows the airways and contains chemicals that can cause cancer.

3 The gases given off are acidic.

4 The gases given off contain carbon dioxide.

5 Carbon monoxide binds to red blood cells, which prevents them carrying oxygen / reduces their ability to carry oxygen.

6 stimulant / speeds up the body's reactions, makes the heart beat faster, narrows blood vessels

Support

Carbon monoxide	Tar	Nicotine
a poisonous gas	a sticky, black material	is addictive
stops blood cells carrying oxygen	damages your lungs	a stimulant
	contains chemicals that cause cancer	makes the heart beat faster

B4 Plants

B4.1 Photosynthesis

Risk assessment

Risk assessments should include any hazards connected with the practical, and sensible precautions (actions) to take to reduce the hazard. For example:

Hazard/Risk	Safety measure taken to manage hazard/risk	Action needed in case of injury or contact with hazardous substance
iodine (irritant)	wear safety glasses	wash off skin
Bunsen burner	tie long hair back	run cold water over burned skin
ethanol (flammable / burns easily)	keep away from open flames	clean up any spills

Questions

1 a description of how iodine turned blue–black when added to the prepared leaf
2 Iodine is a test for starch. If iodine turns blue–black, starch is present. Therefore, the leaf contains starch from stored glucose produced through photosynthesis.
3 carbon dioxide + water $\xrightarrow{\text{sunlight}}$ glucose + oxygen

B4.2 Leaves

Results

Your diagram should include at least one labelled stoma (credit the plural, stomata, being used) with guard cells around it. Examples of labels: stoma – hole that allows gases to diffuse into and out of the leaf; guard cells – cells that open and close the stomata.

Questions

1 carbon dioxide
2 photosynthesis, to produce glucose (and oxygen)
3 oxygen and water vapour
4

Adaptation	Function
green	*chlorophyll absorbs (takes in) sunlight*
thin	*allows gases to diffuse into and out of the leaf easily*
large surface area	absorb as much light as possible
veins	*contain vessels to transport water and glucose*
waxy layer	reduce water loss

Support

1 A – guard cells; B – stoma (plural: stomata)
2 Guard cells **open** and **close** the stomata. A single stomata is called a stoma. When the stoma is open, **carbon dioxide** diffuses into the leaf where it is used for photosynthesis. **Oxygen** (produced by photosynthesis) and water vapour diffuse from the leaf, through the stomata, and out into the environment.
3 1 green – **D**. chlorophyll absorbs (takes in) sunlight
  2 thin – **B**. allows gases to diffuse into and out of the leaf easily
  3 large surface area – **E**. absorb (take in) as much light as possible
  4 veins – **C**. contain vessels to transport water and glucose
  5 waxy layer – **A**. reduce water loss

B4.3 Plant minerals

Questions

1 The seedlings grown in fertilizer are taller / have more leaves / have bigger leaves than the seedlings grown with water. (Answers will depend on the variable you chose to measure.)
2 The fertilizer provides the best/greater levels of nutrients, and so enables the plants to photosynthesize at a greater rate so they grow more quickly.
3 Check fertilizer packets used; most will contain nitrates, phosphates, and potassium.

4 Completed table as follows:

Mineral	Function in plants	Symptoms of deficiency
nitrates	healthy growth	poor growth older leaves are yellowed
phosphates	healthy roots	poor root growth younger leaves look purple
magnesium	making chlorophyll	leaves will turn yellow

B4.4 Flowers and pollination

Questions

Task 1

1

Part of the flower	Function
sepal	protects the flower bud
petal	attracts insects
filament	holds the anther up
anther	makes the pollen
stigma	sticky for pollen to attach to
style	holds the stigma above the ovary
ovary	contains the egg cell

2 The transfer of pollen from the anther to the stigma.

Task 2

Structure	Insect-pollinated	Wind-pollinated
petal size	large	small
petal colour	bright	green or brown
nectar (sweet liquid) produced?	yes	no
pollen type	sticky	low mass
amount of pollen produced	small amounts	large amounts
attachment of anthers and stigmas	fixed, within the flower	loose, hang out of the flower

Support

1 **1** carpel – **D**
2 petal – **C**
3 sepal – **B**
4 stamen – **A**

2 carpel (female): stigma, style, ovary
stamen (male): anther, filament

3 pollen

4 stigma

B4.5 Fertilization and germination

Questions

Task 1

1 seed coat: cover on the outside to protect the seed
embryo: young root and shoot that will develop into an adult plant
food store: used by the plant until it can make its own food by photosynthesis

2 ovary

3 fertilized ovule

4 Any three from (in the correct order):
The pollen grain lands on the stigma.
The pollen grain grows a tube (down the style into the ovary).
The pollen nucleus travels down the tube.
The pollen nucleus joins with the nucleus of the ovule.

Task 2

1 Results are likely to show that low levels of water result in low germination rates; medium water levels have good germination rates; high water levels have low germination rates. Therefore, medium water levels are best for germination.

2 Any three from (in the correct order):
The seed absorbs water.
The seed coat splits.
The root grows down and the shoot grows up.
Leaves appear.

Support

Task 1

1 1 seed coat – **B**. cover on the outside to protect the seed
2 embryo – **C**. young root and shoot that will develop into an adult plant
3 food store – **A**. used by the plant until it can make its own food by photosynthesis

2 The pollen grain lands on the stigma.
The pollen grain grows a tube (down the style into the ovary).
The pollen nucleus travels down the tube.
The pollen nucleus joins with the nucleus of the ovule.

Task 2

1 Your results.

2 Answer will depend on your results.

3 The seed absorbs **water**, causing the seed **coat** to split. The **root** grows down and the **shoot** grows up. Finally, **leaves** appear and the plant can start to make its own food.

B4.6 Seed dispersal

Questions

1 Wing length
2 Distance seed travelled
3 Any two from: height from which seed is dropped; wind speed/air movement; mass attached to seed; wing width
4 Correct length identified – this should be the longest tested
5 The further the seed is carried, the less competition it is likely to have from its parent plant/other seeds for nutrients/water.

Support

1 The **independent** variable is wing size of the seeds.
The **dependent** variable is distance the seed travels.
The **control** variable is the height the seed is dropped.
2 Your results
3 Your calculations
4 Correct length identified – this should be the longest tested

C1 Particles and their behaviour

C1.1 The particle model

Task

The silver ring would have different properties from those of the gold ring because it is made up of different particles.

The ice cube would have different properties from those of liquid water. In liquid water, particles move over each other. In an ice cube, the particles do not move around.

Questions

1 The properties of a substance depend on the following: the shape and size of the particles; how its particles are arranged; how its particles move; how strongly its particles are held together.

2

Sentence starters	Sentence finisher
1 Materials are made of =	B particles.
2 In a substance, all the particles are =	D the same.
3 Different substances are made of =	A different particles.
4 The properties of a substance are due to the =	C particles it is made from.

3 It is not a substance because it is made of more than one type of particle. A substance has only one type of particle.

C1.2 States of matter

Results

	Solid state	Liquid state	Gas state
Particle diagrams	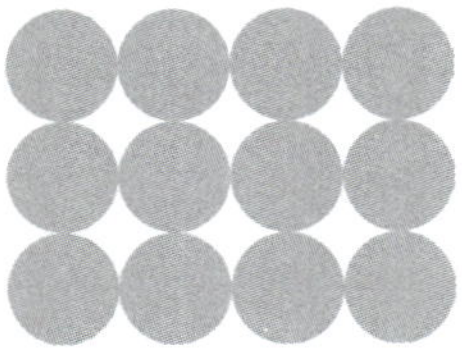	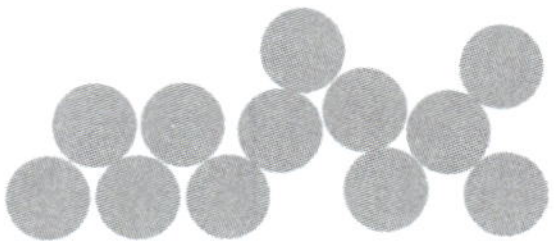	
Arrangement of particles	in a pattern	no pattern	no pattern
Distance between particles	touching their neighbours	touching their neighbours	far apart
Movement of particles	vibrate (shake) on the spot	moving over each other in different directions	quickly and in every direction

Table 1

State of matter	Solid	Liquid	Gas
Can you compress the substance?	no	no	yes, a lot
Does the substance flow?	no	yes	yes
Does the substance take the shape of its container?	no, its shape is fixed unless you apply a force	it takes the shape of the bottom of its container	it takes the shape of the whole container

Table 2

Questions

1 When a substance is in the solid state, its particles are arranged in a regular pattern and touch their neighbours. Its particles do not move around; instead, they vibrate (shake) on the spot.

When a substance is in the liquid state, its particles touch their neighbours and move in all directions, from place to place, moving over each other.

In the gas state, particles spread out until they are far apart and move quickly and in all directions, everywhere in the container.

2 **Differences**: In the solid state, a substance cannot flow. In the liquid state, a substance can flow.

In the solid state, a substance does not take the shape of its container. In the liquid state, it will take the shape of the bottom of its container.

Similarity: In both the solid and the liquid states, a substance cannot be compressed (pressed into a smaller shape).

3 Substances in the liquid state cannot be compressed. However, in the gas state they can be compressed a lot.

Substances in both the liquid and the gas states can flow.

4 **a** Ice cannot be compressed because its particles are touching in a fixed position.

b Water can flow in the liquid state because its particles are free to move over each other.

c Water vapour takes the shape of its container in the gas state because its particles move quickly and in all directions, everywhere in the container.

C1.3 Density

Questions

1 **a** the amount of matter in an object
  b the amount of space an object takes up
  c the mass of a substance in a certain volume
2 what the particles of aluminium are like
3 Aluminium particles have a smaller mass than iron particles.
4 how its particles are arranged and separated (their distance apart)
5 Aluminium particles are slightly closer together in the solid state than they are in the liquid state.
6 Aluminium particles are much closer together in the liquid state than they are in the gas state.

Support

Key word		Definitions
1 mass	=	**A** the amount of matter in an object
2 volume	=	**C** the amount of space an object takes up
3 density	=	**B** the mass of a substance in a certain volume

C1.4 Melting and freezing

1 How strongly its particles hold together
2 As a substance melts, the arrangement of its particles become random (irregular), and they get slightly further apart. The particles start to move around more and move past one another.
3 The temperature decreases steadily until 100 °C where it levels off for some time. The temperature then decreases steadily again until 0 °Cl where it levels off for some time. The temperature then decreases steadily again.
4 0 °C

Support

2 As a substance melts, the arrangement of its particles becomes **irregular**. The particles start to move around **more** and **move past one another**.

C1.5 Boiling

1 The line increases steadily until it reaches 100 °C, where it levels off and stops increasing.
2 100 °C
3 The boiling point is the temperature where the substance remains at the same temperature for a period of time as it is being heated.
4 liquid and gas
5 **a** solid
  b gas

6 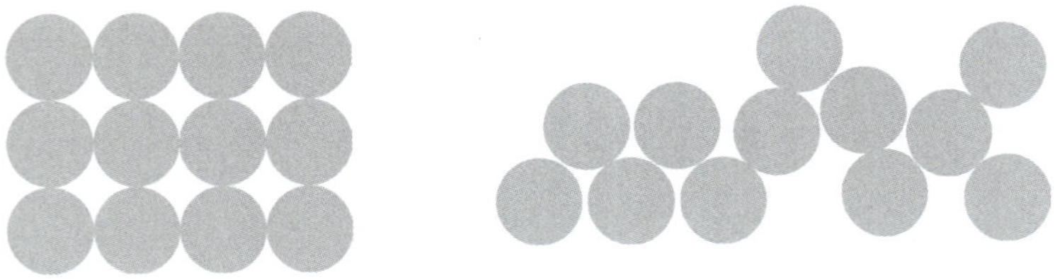

7 The particle arrangement stays random (irregular). However, the particles move much further apart, and move faster in all directions.

C1.6 More changes of state

1 a liquid → gas
   b gas → liquid
   c solid → gas

2 Describing changes of state:
   a When alcohol hand gel evaporates, the arrangement of particles remains irregular, but the particles get much further apart, and move faster in all directions.
   b When water condenses, the arrangement of the particles remains irregular, but the particles get much closer together and touch, moving past each other in all directions.
   c When carbon dioxide sublimes, the arrangement of the particles goes from regular to irregular, and the particles move much further apart and no longer touch. Instead, they move in all directions.

3 Venn diagram for evaporating and boiling:

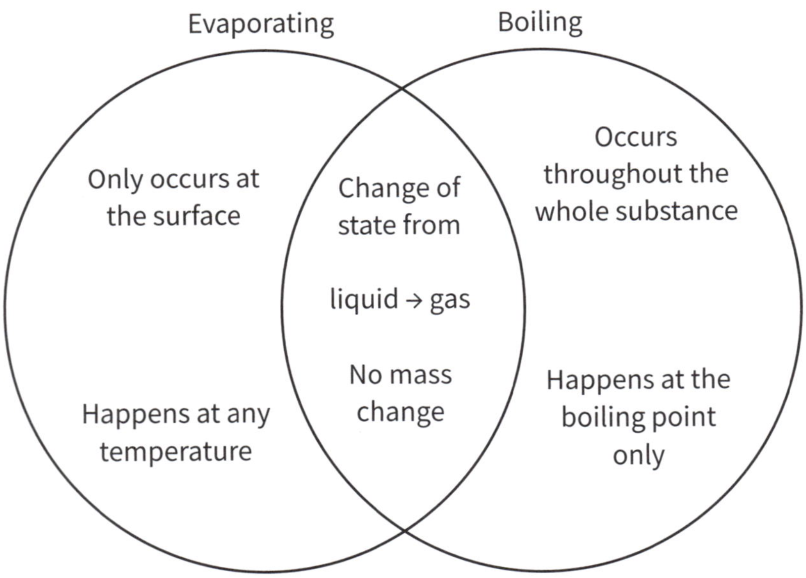

4 There is no difference in the changes in the arrangement, separation (distance apart), and movement of the particles in evaporating and boiling. However, evaporation only occurs with the particles at the surface of the liquid, and boiling happens throughout the whole of the substance.

C1.7 Diffusion

1 higher temperature
2 To ensure the water is not mixed, which would affect the results.
3 The tea particles spread out to fill the beaker.
4 Factors affecting diffusion:
  a Temperature – At higher temperatures, particles are moving faster, so diffusion happens faster.
  b Particle size – The bigger and heavier the particle, the slower it diffuses.
  c State – Particles cannot diffuse in the solid state, as the particles do not move. Particles can diffuse in both the gas and the liquid states.
5 The particles are moving faster in the beaker of hot water. Therefore, diffusion of the tea particles will happen more quickly.

C2 Elements, atoms, and compounds

C2.1 Elements

1 elements
2 Elements with similar properties are grouped together.
3 An element is a substance that cannot be broken down into other substances.
4 a C H I P S
  b F Li C K
  c S H I P
  d P H Y Si Cs
  e Ba Na Na
  f S Li N K Y
  g Sc Ar Er
  h Ge Ni U S
  i Dy N Am I Te
  j He Li Co Pt Er
5 a phosphorus iodine radium tellurium
  b molybdenum uranium selenium
  c lutetium carbon potassium yttrium
  d fluorine lanthanum sulfur hydrogen
  e vanadium iodine oxygen lithium nitrogen

Support

1 An element is a substance that cannot be broken down into other substances.
2 The Periodic Table shows … all the known elements, grouped together with elements with similar properties.

3

hydrogen	H	nickel	Ni
helium	He	germanium	Ge
lithium	Li	selenium	Se
carbon	C	yttrium	Y
nitrogen	N	molybdenum	Mo
oxygen	O	tellurium	Te
fluorine	F	iodine	I
sodium	Na	caesium	Cs
silicon	Si	barium	Ba
phosphorous	P	lanthanum	La
sulfur	S	platinum	Pt
argon	Ar	dysprosium	Dy
potassium	K	erbium	Er
scandium	Sc	uranium	U
vanadium	V	americium	Am
cobalt	Co		

C2.2 Atoms

Task

1 element, the same, different, properties, colour

2 a = several atoms from one element only; b = several atoms from one element only; c = lots of atoms from two different elements; d = an individual atom

3 hydrogen atoms = diagram b; iron atoms = diagram a
The atoms in diagram b are smaller than the atoms in diagram a, so b must be hydrogen.

Questions

1 one

2 two

3 no

4 600 000 000 000 000 000 000 000

C2.3 Compounds

Results

Observations	Iron	Sulfur	Iron sulfide
Does the bulb light?	yes	no	no
Is it attracted to the bar magnet?	yes	no	no
What does the substance look like?	silver/grey	yellow	grey
What state is this substance in?	solid	solid	solid

Questions

1 A compound is a substance that is made up of atoms of two or more elements, strongly joined together.
2 Iron will allow a bulb to light and is magnetic, but iron sulfide is neither of these.
3 The particles are all different.
4 Images A and C show an element because they only show one type of atom. Image B shows a compound because it shows more than one element joined together.

Support

1 A compound is a substance that ... is made up of atoms of two or more elements, strongly joined together.
2 Iron sulfide particles are **different from** iron particles.
3 This diagram shows a compound because it is made up of atoms of two elements = B.
This diagram shows an element because it has atoms of only one type = A and C.

C2.4 Chemical formulae

1

Compound name	Description
1 sulfur dioxide	C one sulfur atom and two oxygen atoms
2 sulfur monoxide	D one sulfur atom and one oxygen atom
3 carbon monoxide	A one carbon atom and one oxygen atom
4 carbon dioxide	B one carbon atom and two oxygen atoms

2 **a** two hydrogen atoms and one oxygen atom
b two chlorine atoms
c one sodium atom and one chlorine atom
d one nitrogen atom and three hydrogen atoms
3 **a** sulfur trioxide
b nitrogen monoxide
4 **a** H_2O
b H_2
c O_2
5 ZnO
6 SO_3

C3 The Periodic Table

C3.1 Three elements

Questions

1 Non-metal elements are found on the right side of the Periodic Table.
2 **a** shiny, easy to shape into thin sheets, good conductor of electricity
b not shiny/dull, poor conductor of electricity, brittle (breaks easily)
c shiny, brittle, can change the direction of light

3 **a** in electricity cables
b to make fertilizers
c in fibre-optic cables
4 Copper is easily shaped into thin sheets, but sulfur is brittle.
5 Copper is easily shaped into thin sheets, but germanium is brittle.
6 Germanium is shiny, but sulfur is dull.
7 Copper is a good conductor of electricity, making it suitable for use in electricity cables.

Support

1

Element	Property
1 copper	A shiny; B. good conductor of electricity; D. easy to shape into thin sheets
2 sulfur	C poor conductor of electricity; E. brittle (breaks easily); F. (dull (not shiny))
3 germanium	A shiny; E. brittle (breaks easily); G. can change the direction of light

2

Element	Use
1 Copper	C used in electricity cables
2 Sulfur	B used to make fertilizers
3 Germanium	A used in fibre-optic cables

C3.2 Physical properties of metals and non-metals

1 any **four** from: conductor of electricity, good conductor of heat, shiny, high density, malleable (can be shaped easily without breaking), sonorous
2 any **four** from: poor conductor of electricity, poor conductor of heat, dull (not shiny), low density, brittle (breaks easily), not sonorous
3 metalloids
4 Physical properties are the properties you can see, feel, or measure without changing the material.
5 Metal elements are on the left side of the Periodic Table.
6 Non-metal elements are on the right side of the Periodic Table.
7 Metal: sodium, iron, nickel
Non-metal: fluorine, nitrogen

Support

1

Properties of a typical metal (when solid)	Properties of a typical non-metal (when solid)
conductor of electricity	**poor conductor of electricity**
good conductor of heat	poor conductor of heat
shiny	dull (not shiny)
high density	**low density**
malleable (can be shaped easily without breaking)	brittle (breaks easily)
sonorous (rings when hit)	**not sonorous**

2 (1.) Physical properties are … (B.) … the properties you can see, feel, or measure without changing the material.
3 (1.) Metals … (B.) are on the left side of the Periodic Table.
(2.) Non-metals … (A.) are on the right side of the Periodic Table.

C3.3 Chemical properties of metals and non-metals

Results

Reaction	Observation of colour change	Is the solution acidic or alkaline?
magnesium + oxygen	The silver metal turns into a white powder.	X
sulfur + oxygen	The yellow powder turns brown/darker.	X
carbon dioxide + water	The universal indicator solution turns pink/red.	acidic
magnesium oxide + water	Red litmus paper turns blue/purple.	alkaline

Questions

1 The chemical properties of a substance describe its chemical reactions.
2 magnesium oxide
3 magnesium + oxygen → magnesium oxide
4 The red litmus paper would turn blue.
5 alkaline
6 Typical metals react with oxygen to form a metal oxide. This forms an alkaline solution when dissolved in water.
7 sulfur dioxide
8 sulfur + oxygen → sulfur dioxide
9 The universal indicator would turn pink/red.
10 acidic
11 Typical non-metals react with oxygen to form a non-metal oxide. This forms an acidic solution when dissolved in water.

Support

1 (1.) Chemical properties of a substance… (C.) describe its chemical reactions.
2 (1.) Metals… (B.) react with oxygen to make a metal oxide.
(2.) Non-metals… (A.) react with oxygen to make a non-metal oxide.

C3.4 Groups and periods

1 groups
2 periods
3 **a** Group 4, Period 2
b Group 1, Period 3
c Group 0, Period 1
d Group 5, Period 2
e Group 2, Period 3
f Group 7, Period 3
4 **a** hydrogen
b lithium
c calcium
d aluminium
e neon
5 **a** The density of the elements **increases** as you go down the group.
b any number between 4.6 and 13.2 inclusive
6 The density of the elements in the group increases from top to bottom.

C3.5 The elements of Group 1

1 Group 1 elements are metals.
2 Group 1 elements are on the left side of the Periodic Table, with the metals.
3 hydrogen

4 good conductors of electricity, good conductors of heat, shiny when freshly cut
5 any **two** from: lower melting points than other metals, lower boiling points than other metals, softer than other metals
6 The reactions of Group 1 elements with water get **more** vigorous (strong) as you go down the group.
7 The reaction of rubidium with water will be more vigorous than the reaction with potassium.
8 a sodium + water → sodium hydroxide + hydrogen
b potassium + water → potassium hydroxide + water
9 a

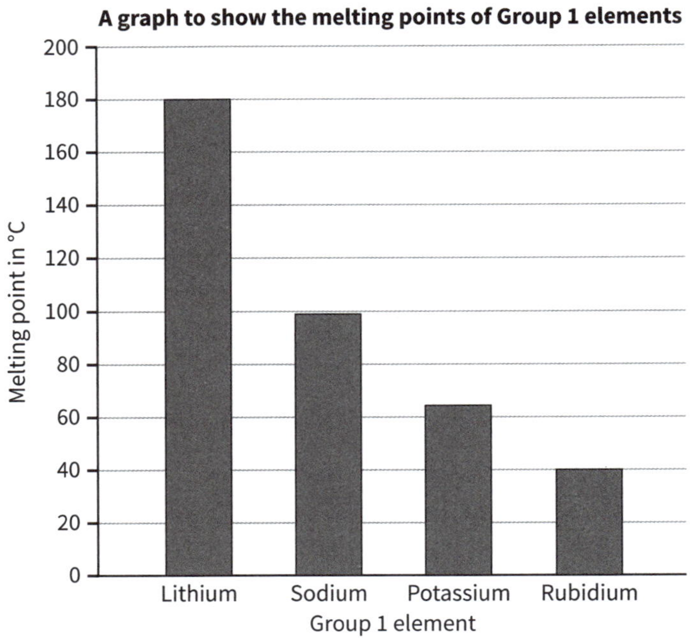

b The melting points of Group 1 elements **decrease** as you go down the group.
10 The boiling points of Group 1 elements **decrease** as you go down the group.

Support

1 The physical properties of Group 1 elements are: soft, shiny, lower melting points than other metals, good conductors of heat and electricity.
2 The melting points of Group 1 elements **decrease** as you go down the group.
The boiling points of Group 1 elements **decrease** as you go down the group.

C3.6 The elements of Group 7

Task

Group 7 element	Colour	State at room temperature	Melting point in °C	Boiling point in °C	Reactive or unreactive?	Product when reacted with iron
chlorine	pale green	gas	−101	−35	reactive	iron chloride
bromine	dark red	liquid	−7	59	reactive	iron bromine
iodine	grey	solid	114	184	reactive	iron iodide

Questions

1 At room temperature, chlorine is a pale green gas, bromine is a dark red liquid, and iodine is a grey solid.
2 Group 7 elements have low melting points.
3 The melting points of the Group 7 elements increase as you go down the group.
4 The boiling points of the Group 7 elements increase as you go down the group.
5 **a** Group 7 elements react similarly with iron to form an iron halide.
  b iron + iodide → iron iodide
  c iron bromide
6 The reactions of the Group 7 elements get less vigorous (strong) as you go down the group.

Support

1

Group 7 element	Colour	State at room temperature
chlorine =	pale green =	gas
bromine =	dark red =	liquid
iodine =	grey =	solid

2 The melting points of the Group 7 elements increase as you go down the group.
3 The boiling points of the Group 7 elements increase as you go down the group.

C3.7 The elements of Group 0

Task

Your bar chart should have correctly plotted data with a suitable scale on the *y*-axis, with equally spaced intervals, and correctly labelled axes ('Boiling point in °C' on the *y*-axis and 'Element' on the *x*-axis). Bars should also be evenly spaced with gaps in between them.

Questions

1 The noble gases are in Group 0, on the far-right side of the Periodic Table.
2 The Group 0 elements are all **unreactive**, and they get **more** reactive as you go down the group.
3 They do not take part in many reactions.
4 The Group 0 elements are colourless substances in the gas state at room temperature, and they have low melting and boiling points.
5

Group 0	Common use
1 helium	B in balloons
2 argon	C in the space between sheets of glass in aa double-glazed windows
3 neon	A in light-up advertising signs

6 Helium has a lower density than air, so it is used in balloons. Argon is a better thermal insulator than air, so it is used in the space between glass sheets in double-glazed windows. Neon glows brightly when high-voltage electricity passes through it, so it is used in advertising signs.
7 As you go down the group, the boiling points of the Group 0 elements increase.
8 As you go down the group, the melting points of the Group 0 elements increase.

Support

1 **a** The Group 0 elements are all colourless substances in the gas state at room temperature.

b The Group 0 elements have low melting and boiling points.

2 (1.) As you go down the group, the melting points of the Group 0 elements … (A.) increase.

(2.) As you go down the group, the boiling points of the Group 0 elements … (A.) increase.

C4 Acids and alkalis

C4.1 Acids and alkalis

Task

Old hazard symbol	New hazard symbol	Name	Description
		toxic	This can be poisonous and possibly cause death.
		flammable	This can catch fire easily.
		health hazard (harmful)	This contains dangerous organisms such as bacteria.
		caution (irritant)	This includes irritants, harmful (dangerous) substances, and some low-hazard substances.
		corrosive	This may dissolve or burn materials, including skin.
		explosive	This may explode.

Questions

1 (1.) A hazard is … (B.) anything that can cause you harm (hurt you).

(2.) A hazard symbol is … (A.) an image used to give information about the dangers of a chemical.

2 **a** corrosive

b can burn your skin, can burn or damage your eyes

c Wear safety glasses/goggles. Do not touch the solutions.

Support

1 See table under task (above).

2 can burn your skin; can burn or damage your eyes

3 Wear goggles/safety glasses; Do not touch the solutions.

C4.2 Indicators and pH

1 red
2 blue
3

Range	Solution
1 a pH of more than 7	B alkaline
2 a pH of less than 7	C acidic
3 a pH of 7	A neutral

4 D, A, C, B
5 A, B, and D
6 E
7 C and F
8 using a pH probe / pH meter

Applications of pH testing

1 a pH 9 b pH 5 c pH 11
2 Field 2

C4.3 Neutralization

1 any four from: the amount of indigestion remedy, the size of the beakers, the type of acid being added, the type of indigestion remedy, the number of drops of indicator, the number of drops of acid being added
2 the type of indigestion remedy
3 number of drops of acid being added to neutralize the remedy
4 any **two** from: the amount of indigestion remedy, the size of the beakers, the type of acid being added, the number of drops of indicator
5 The universal indicator will turn green.
6 a substance that neutralizes an acid
7 a base that dissolves / a soluble base
8 a reaction where an acid reacts with a substance to cancel it out
9 pH of below 7
10 pH of above 7
11 pH of 7
12 The pH increased.
13 any **two** from: adding base to over-acidic soil to increase the pH, using alkaline toothpaste to brush teeth after eating and drinking, putting vinegar on an alkaline wasp sting to decrease the pH, adding base to acidic lakes to increase the pH
14 indigestion remedy B
15 Indigestion remedy B required more acid to neutralize it, so it would neutralize more acid in the stomach.

Support

1

Type of variable	Experiment
1 independent variable	B type of indigestion remedy
2 dependent variable being measured	C number of drops of acid being added
3 control variable being kept the same	A type of acid being added

2 **Key word** — **Definition**

Key word	Definition
1 base	C a substance that neutralizes an acid
2 alkali	B a base that dissolves
3 neutralization	A a reaction where an acid reacts with a substance to cancel it out

3 Examples of neutralization reactions: adding base to over-acidic soil to increase the pH; using alkaline toothpaste to brush teeth after eating and drinking; putting vinegar on an alkaline wasp sting to decrease the pH; adding base to acidic lakes to increase the pH

C4.4 Making salts

1 magnesium and hydrochloric acid
2 magnesium chloride and hydrogen
3 magnesium + hydrochloric acid → magnesium chloride + hydrogen
4 neutral
5 neutralization
6 a compound that forms when an acid reacts with a metal element or compound
7 calcium chloride
8 sodium nitrate
9 Add hydrochloric acid to a beaker; add magnesium oxide powder to the beaker and mix; keep adding the magnesium oxide until some is left over; filter to remove the extra, unreacted magnesium oxide; heat the solution in an evaporating basin until half of the water evaporates; leave the evaporating basin in a warm place to allow the rest of the water to evaporate and the crystals to form.

Support

1 (1.) A salt is … (B.) a compound that forms when an acid reacts with a metal element or compound.
2 calcium chloride, sodium nitrate
3 C – A – E – B – F – D

P1 Forces

P1.1 Introduction to forces

1 depends on readings
2 Hold the newton meter, string, and object in a straight line and take the reading perpendicular (at right angles) to the scale.

P1.2 Squashing and stretching

1 The pattern depends on your measurements and results. Expect:
- as force increases, length/extension of spring increases
- as force doubles, extension doubles
- force is directly proportional to the extension.

Use of data from your table to explain your conclusion.
2 depends on predictions and results

3 any **one** from: use a pointer to measure the bottom of the spring; make sure the metre ruler is perpendicular (at right angles) to the bench; fix the metre rule to the clamp stand; use more weights; repeat results; calculate the mean

P1.3 Drag forces and friction

1 depends on results – The surface with the most friction should have the largest force needed to start moving the object.
2 depends on results – The surface with the least friction should have the smallest force needed to start moving the object.
3 depends on predictions and results
4 any **two** from: mass of object; type of sole on shoe; surface area/size of sole on shoe; angle of surface
5 any **one** from: check for zero error on the newton meter; repeat results; calculate the mean
6 any **one** from: zero error on newton meter; newton meter not horizontal / parallel to surface; shoe starts to lift up off surface
7 Two objects in contact have uneven surfaces. This causes friction and makes it more difficult for the objects to move past each other.

P1.4 Forces at a distance

1 (approximately) 1 Newton
2 Mass is the amount of matter/stuff in an object and is measured in kilogram. Weight is the force of gravity acting on an object and is measured in newtons.
3 Weight is mass multiplied by 10 (approximately).
4 weight (in Newton) = mass (in kilogram) × gravitational field strength (in N/kilogram)
5 any **one** from: check for zero error on the newton meter; repeat results and calculate the mean; check the value of each mass is accurate using the balance
6 6 × 10
weight = 15 N
7 1200 g = 1.2 kg
weight = mass × 10 or weight = 1.2 × 10
weight = 12 N

P1.5 Balanced and unbalanced

1 constant speed or stay still
2 speed up/accelerate or slow down/decelerate
3 If an object is in equilibrium, the forces acting on it are balanced and so cancel each other out.

P2 Sound

P2.1 Waves

1 up and down
2 up and down
3 back and forth
4 They reflect.
5 vibration, energy
6 The cork moves up and down, but it does not move across the ripple tank.

P2.2 Sound

1 They all vibrate.
2 Students represent the particles; students 'jiggle/move about' to represent the particles vibrating and passing on the sound wave.
3 **Solids:** particles are in a regular arrangement in rows, touching each other.
Liquids: particles are touching each other, but not in rows.
Gases: there are very few particles, well spaced out.

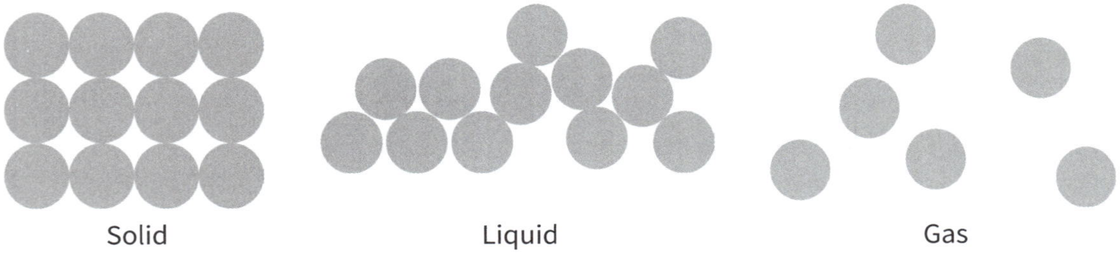

4 **a** 340 m/s
b aluminium
c solids
d A = liquid, B = solid, C = gas

P2.3 Loudness and pitch

1 **a** amplitude
b large amplitude
2 **a** frequency
b high frequency
3 **a** hertz / Hz
b decibels / dB
4 Wave C has the highest pitch because it has the highest frequency.
Wave A has the lowest pitch because it has the lowest frequency.
5 Wave D has the louder sound because it has the bigger amplitude.

P2.4 Detecting sound

1 a A = pinna, B = auditory canal, C = eardrum, D = cochlea, E = auditory nerve
  b auditory canal: directs sound to the eardrum
  auditory nerve: transfers (moves) the electrical signal to the brain
  cochlea: contains fluid (liquid) and hairs that produce an electrical signal
  eardrum: vibrates and passes vibrations to the ossicles
  pinna: directs sound to the auditory canal
  c outer ear: auditory canal, eardrum, pinna; inner ear: cochlea
2 a bat
  b elephant
  c howler monkey
  d cat, bat
  e their hearing range is 117 000 Hz, while other animals have a smaller hearing range.
3 a A = sound waves, B = magnet, C = diaphragm
  b sound, eardrum, cochlea

P2.5 Echoes and ultrasound

Echoes

1 An echo is a sound that reflects off a surface.
2 a any **one** from: to determine (work out) distances; to produce images of human organs and glands, such as the thyroid gland; to identify cracks (breaks) in machinery; to identify heart conditions (echocardiogram)
  b any **one** from: in a recording studio, theatre, or concert hall
3 a Empty rooms have lots of hard, smooth surfaces, which are good at reflecting sound.
  b Carpets and curtains are usually soft and rough. These surfaces are bad at reflecting sound / good at absorbing (taking in) sound.

Using echoes to calculate a distance

4 any **two** from: so bats/dolphins can find their food / detect what is around them; to determine how far away an object is; to determine how deep the ocean is / how far away the seabed is
5 Bats and dolphins use the reflection of ultrasound to find food and to detect what is around them, so that they do not collide with (hit) other objects.
6 A transmitter on a boat sends a pulse (beam) of ultrasound towards the seabed. The pulse is reflected off the seabed. A receiver detects the pulse and uses the speed of ultrasound and the time taken to receive the pulse to determine the depth of the seabed.

Uses of ultrasound

7 Ultrasound is high frequency sound above 20 000 Hz.
8 any **three** from: medical scanning and imaging; to break up kidney stones; in physiotherapy to reduce pain and swelling of damaged tendons; to measure the speed and direction of blood flow
9 A transmitter sends pulses (beams) of ultrasound into a woman's stomach. The ultrasound reflects off the unborn baby and a receiver detects the reflected pulses. A computer is used to build up an image of the unborn baby from the reflected pulse.

P3 Light

P3.1 Light

1 1a–2a: depend on which materials were used and results

2 **b** For example: the cardboard did not completely block the light, the room was lighter for set 2, the lamp was not the same distance away from the light meter.

c The results were/were not precise because my repeat readings were/were not similar.

3 (Support answers: 1 -B -i; 2 -C -ii; 3 -A -iii)

Word	Example	Meaning
transparent	a clear glass window	a see-through material that transmits most light
translucent	a frosted glass window	a material that transmits light but it is scattered as it passes through
opaque	a piece of metal	a material that does not transmit light

4 **a** The Sun

b The ball

c It is absorbed by your eye.

5 **a** Light-time is **distance** measured in terms of how far light travels in a given time. A light-minute is the **distance** light travels in one minute. A light-**year** is the **distance** light travels in one year.

b Distances in space are very large.

P3.2 Reflection

1 **a** The independent variable is the angle of incidence.

b The dependent variable is the angle of reflection.

2 The angle of incidence is the same as the angle of reflection.

3 any **one** from: repeat results and calculate the mean, or discard anomalies; use a thinner light ray; use a dark room; use a brighter light ray

4 The law of reflection states that the angle of incidence is equal to the angle of reflection.

5 3 ray box = A; 1 incident ray = B; 2 normal = C; 4 reflected ray = D

6 Specular reflection is when light rays in one direction meet a smooth surface and are all reflected in one direction. Diffuse scattering is when light rays meet a rough surface and are reflected in all different directions.

7 The light rays from the object are reflected by the mirror and obey the law of reflection. Our brain uses the fact that light travels in straight lines. If the reflected rays are extended as straight lines behind the mirror, they meet at a point where the image is.

8 any **two** from: same shape and size, virtual, same distance behind the mirror as the object is in front of the mirror, laterally inverted

P3.3 Refraction

1 The ray of light does not change direction / stays travelling in the same direction.

2 air to glass: refracts towards the normal

glass to air: refracts away from the normal

3 air to glass: slows down in the glass

glass to air: speeds up in the air

4 a = 3 normal

b = 1 ray box

c = 2 incident ray

d = 4 refracted ray

5

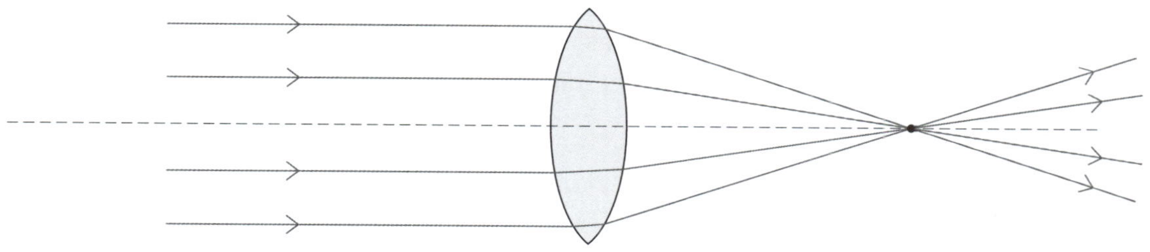

P3.4 The eye and the camera

1 A = ray, B = lens, C = aperture, D = shutter, E = (photographic) film

2 A = optic nerve, B = retina, C = cornea, D = pupil, E = lens, F = object / tree

3 any **three** from: lens, photosensitive surface (retina / film), (shutter / eyelid), pupil / aperture

4 The lens focuses light onto the retina to produce an image of what you see. The image is inverted and real. The retina is a photosensitive material that contains photoreceptors. When light hits the photoreceptors, chemical reactions produce an electrical impulse that travels up the optic nerve to your brain.

P3.5 Colour

White light

1 a The white light refracts at the air to glass and glass to air boundaries. It disperses (spreads out) into a continuous spectrum of colours.

b Different colours refract by different amounts because they have different wavelengths.

Combining colours

2 b

Primary colours mixed	Actual colour produced	Secondary or tertiary?
red and green	*yellow*	*secondary*
red and blue	*magenta*	*secondary*
blue and green	*cyan*	*secondary*

Filters

3 **c** [top to bottom of 'Actual' column] red, black, black, black, blue, black, black, black, green

d A coloured filter only lets through its own colour of light. All other colours are absorbed by the filter.

Coloured objects

4 **d** [top to bottom of 'Actual' column] red, black, black, black, blue, black, black, black, green

e A blue jumper only reflects the blue light in white light. All other colours are absorbed (taken in) by the blue jumper.

f A red hat will look black in blue light. A red hat only reflects red light. There is no red to reflect in the blue light. The blue light is absorbed by the hat, so the hat does not reflect any light and appears black.

g A coloured object appears black unless the object is the same colour as the coloured light. If this is the case, the object will appear the same colour as the coloured light. In white light, the object will appear its true colour as it will reflect this colour and absorb all other colours contained in the white light.

P4 Motion and pressure

P4.1 Speed

1 **a** For example: The repeats are similar to the average in all my activities, so my results are precise.

b tape measure; description of use, such as: laid the tape measure on the floor and marked a start and end point in chalk/tape, or measured distance between pre-marked lines on a court

stopwatch; description of use, such as: counted down before start / stood where could clearly see start and finish point

2 average speed (m/s) $= \dfrac{\text{total distance (m)}}{\text{total time taken (s)}}$

$= \dfrac{240}{40}$

$= 6$ (*m/s*) with correct units

3 average speed (m/s) $= \dfrac{\text{total distance (m)}}{\text{total time taken (s)}}$

$= \dfrac{240}{40}$

$= 6$ (m/s) with correct units

4 The trains have a relative motion of 90 + 50 = 140 km/h to each other.

5 The runners have a relative motion of 9 − 8 = 1 m/s to each other.

P4.2 Motion graphs

1 graph plotted as shown

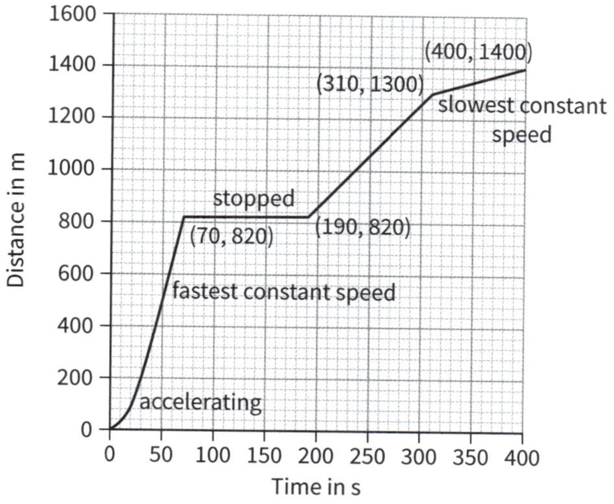

2 each area labelled correctly (as shown in graph above): moving at the slowest constant (steady) speed, accelerating, not moving, moving at the fastest constant speed

3 $\text{average speed (m/s)} = \frac{\text{total distance (m)}}{\text{total time taken (s)}}$

$= \frac{1400}{400}$

$= 3.5$ m/s

4 distance = 860 m

$\text{average speed (m/s)} = \frac{\text{total distance (m)}}{\text{total time taken (s)}}$

$= \frac{860}{200}$

$= 3.5$ m/s

5 distance = 1400 – 860 = 540 m

$\text{average speed (m/s)} = \frac{\text{total distance (m)}}{\text{total time taken (s)}}$

$= \frac{860}{200}$

$= 3.5$ m/s

P4.3 Pressure in gases

1 the collisions of air particles all around you with your body or other objects
2 As altitude increases, atmospheric pressure decreases.
3 When the temperature of a gas increases, gas pressure increases.
4 When the volume of a gas decreases, gas pressure increases.
5 The hot air caused the pressure inside the collapsing bottle. The pressure on the outside of the bottle was the atmospheric pressure. The pressure on the inside was reduced on cooling because the particles had less kinetic energy, so did not collide with the surface of the bottle as much. The pressure on the inside was less than the atmospheric pressure, so the bottle collapsed.

Support

To start, the bottle is heated. The air molecules inside the bottle **collide** with the inside of the bottle, exerting gas **pressure**. When the bottle is removed from the water bath, the temperature inside the bottle **decreases**, so there are **fewer** collisions between the molecules and the inside of the bottle. As a result, the gas pressure inside the bottle becomes **less/lower** than the atmospheric pressure outside the bottle, which causes the bottle to **collapse**.

P4.4 Pressure in liquids

1 The particles in the liquid collide with (hit) the surface of the submarine, exerting/applying force; the pressure acts in all directions.

2 As you go deeper in a liquid, the pressure increases.

3 Water from A on the left side is a mirror image of the water flowing out of the right side.

Water from B falls between the existing flow and the bottle.

Water from C flows further than the water from the existing flow.

Conclusion

Increasing the **area** of the bottom of the clay allowed the clay to **float**.

This is because it increased the **upthrust** acting on the clay. When the **upthrust** was equal to the **weight**, the clay floated. It is water **pressure** that produces the **upthrust**.

Support

1 When a submarine is underwater, there is a **pressure** acting on it due to the water molecules. This is because of the **collisions** of the water **molecules/particles** on the surface of the submarine. The pressure is exerted (applied) in **all** directions.

2 As you go deeper in a liquid, the pressure **increases**.

P4.5 Pressure on solids

1 a

$$\text{pressure (N/m}^2) = \frac{\text{force (N)}}{\text{area (m}^2)}$$

$$= \frac{650}{0.0104}$$

$$= 62\,500\ \text{N/m}^2$$

b area = 2. × 0.0104 m^2 = 0.0208 m^2

$$\text{pressure (N/m}^2) = \frac{\text{force (N)}}{\text{area (m}^2)}$$

$$= \frac{650}{0.0208}$$

$$= 31\,250\ \text{N/m}^2$$

c When you stand on one foot, the pressure is **greater**. This is because **the same** force is acting over **a smaller** area.

2 Pressure is a measure of the force acting per unit area. It always acts at 90° to the surface.

3 The wide straps **increase** the area in contact with the body. The **force** acts over a **larger** area. This **decreases** the pressure.

4 A sharp knife will have a smaller area in contact with the substance. This means it has a higher pressure for the same applied force.

P4.6 Turning forces

1 When the ruler is balanced, the clockwise (to the right) moment **equals/is the same as** the anticlockwise (to the left) moment.

2 I would push down at **A** because it is **furthest from** the pivot. This would give me the largest **moment/turning force** for the same **force** applied.

3 Moment (Nm) = force (Newton) × distance (m) = 600 × 2 = 1200 Nm

4 If the slope is very steep, the **weight / centre of gravity** might act outside of the base. This would cause the tractor to **tip / topple / be unstable**.